LED BY LOVE

Maria do Carmo Bogo

LED BY LOVE

A missionary Way of the Cross

Illustrations by Marcello Silvestri

Comboni Missionaries
_____
St Paul Publications

Comboni Missionaries
London Road, Sunningdale SL5 0JX, United Kingdom

St Paul Publications
Middlegreen, Slough SL3 6BT, United Kingdom

Copyright © Comboni Missionaries of the Heart of Jesus,
Sunningdale 1990

ISBN 085439 329 3

Printed in Italy by Società San Paolo, Roma

Introduction

The way of the cross is, simply, God's wandering in all our different ways.

He became so much like each one of us that we stumble over him all the time and yet we fail to recognize him. Since that night in which he was born of Mary to walk the ways of the poor, to heal and forgive them, he has never ceased to be a scandal for the "rich" and the "virtuous".

God's identity card shows all names and faces: of the terrorist; of the sick, hungry child dying of deprivation in some remote tribe; of the old person, trapped in a flat, yet striving to give meaning to her devastating loneliness. God bears the horrified angry face of the bereaved parents whose child has been killed in a stupid accident. He wears the school uniform of the teenager continually running away from parental quarrels. We can even imagine him in the tiny limbs of an unborn baby to whom the sacred right of life has been denied. He can be called the son of the unmarried girl living just down the road as well as the Son of the Most High God.

1 | The Son of God is condemned

FIRST STORY
Wisdom 2:12-13;17-20

"Let us lie in wait for the virtuous man, since he annoys us and opposes our way of life, reproaches us for our breaches of the law and accuses us of playing false to our upbringing. He claims to have knowledge of God and calls himself a son of the Lord.

Let us see if what he says is true. Let us observe what kind of end he himself will have. If the virtuous man is God's son, God will take his part and rescue him from the clutches of his enemies. Let us test him with cruelty and with torture, and thus explore this gentleness of his and put his endurance to the test. Let us condemn him to a shameful death since he will be looked after. We have his word for it."

SECOND STORY

THE PROPHET

... Many times God breaks the rules.
He ignores the protocol!
He calls the wrong people
to carry out his right purposes.
He sends children to instruct old men,
shepherds to inform kings,
naked boys to engage battle
against the arms of giants

7

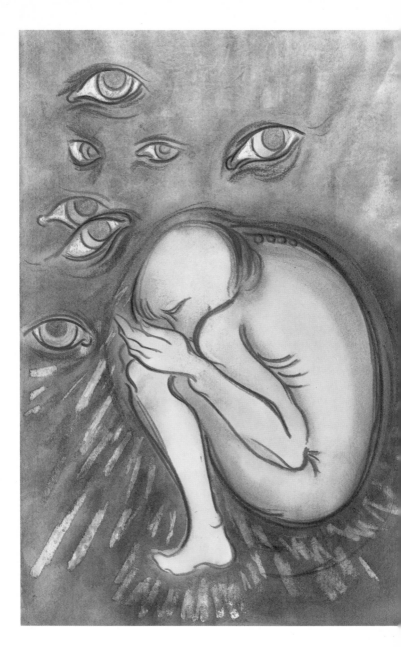

and put them to flight.
The bare foot of the prophet
shall not rest in the royal palaces.
The words of his mouth are much too fresh
to be heard in the closed rooms
full of diplomatic lies.
Fettered in the underground,
he cries for justice;
his voice will never be silent again.
Once more,
God himself, rejected and driven away,
descends into our hell, to comfort the victims
of the democratic systems
and perhaps the so-called "Christian Democracies".
The "respectable" people
can't recognize him,
even if they keep studying
the books of the law every day,
with much reverence,
but without the light of justice.

LET US PRAY

Jesus, help us to see you in our
neighbour whether innocent or
guilty and to stop committing the
same injustices in our world of
today.

ACCLAMATION

**Lord,
by your cross and resurrection
you have set us free;
you are the Saviour of the world.**

2 | The Son of God carries his cross

FIRST STORY
Mark 14:32-37

They came to an olive grove called the garden of Gethsemane and he instructed his disciples, "Sit here while I go and pray."

He took Peter, James and John with him and he began to be filled with horror and deepest distress. And he said to them, "My soul is crushed by sorrow to the point of death; stay here and watch with me."

He went on a little further and fell to the ground and prayed that if it were possible the awful hour awaiting him might never come.

"Father, Father," he said, "everything is possible for you. Take away this cup from me. Yet I want your will not mine." Then he returned to the three disciples and found them asleep.

SECOND STORY

ILLNESS

I've seen
a falling leaf;
she was green
and, suddenly stricken,
she started journeying
towards the ground.

10

A new deep pain
brought the news
of the totally new:
AIDS, cancer, heart disease.
From now onwards,
the earth starts moving underfoot,
and yet
the sky
is too far away to be grasped.

A merciless hurricane
is driving her away,
against all reason,
for the last mile of the journey,
What a long, weary and painful mile...!
What a savage power
thrusting her in a dark direction!

Just a little while and the sick leaf
will fall to the ground;
or... hopefully
she will be carried away
by a merciful wind
into a welcoming
land?!

But the last mile
is bound to be painful.
Needles are to be driven
into the dried up veins,
there,
in a strange place,
surrounded by strangers,
looked upon

as nothing else but
half-dead flesh.

The soul,
deep down,
weeps in a distant place,
yes,
still in the flesh
and yet
so far off
and beyond it...

LET US PRAY

Jesus, give us faith and courage
to unite our sufferings with the
sufferings of our brothers and sisters
without exception, as we pray for all
the peoples of the world that they
may become one with you.

ACCLAMATION

Lord,
by your cross and resurrection
you have set us free;
you are the Saviour of the world.

3 | The Son of God has no strength to go on

FIRST STORY
1 Kings 19:1-4;10

Queen Jezebel sent this message to Elijah, "You killed my prophets, and now I swear by the gods that I'm going to kill you by this time tomorrow night."

So Elijah fled for his life; he went to Beersheba, a city of Judah, and left his servant there. Then he went alone into the wilderness, travelling all day, and sat down under a broom bush and prayed that he might die.

"I've had enough," he told the Lord. "Take away my life. I've got to die sometime, and it might as well be now."... But the Lord said to him, "What are you doing here, Elijah?"

He replied, "I have worked very hard for the Lord God of heavens; but the people of Israel have broken their covenant with you and torn down your altars and killed your prophets, and only I am left; and now they are trying to kill me too."

SECOND STORY

IN A PRISON CELL

The young offender
was locked up in a prison cell,
with a wild heart
whose appeal was too weak

14

against the "lawful" white-washed wall.
Then
emptiness opened a dry cistern underfoot,
and the clouds of fear and loneliness
gathered above
calling the thunder of despair
into that pale narrow sky;
until...
his whole life
was being smashed
against the dirty ceiling
and the bright dreams melted away
in muddy foot-paths.
A last unheard deep cry,
and the bed-sheet
was seen
as the liberating instrument
around the fragile neck.
"Suicide!!!"
the officials cried.
"NO! NO!"
It was killing...

LET US PRAY

    Jesus, forgive us for having applied
    our laws without a vision
    of discernment and respect
    for the human person.

ACCLAMATION

    Lord,
    by your cross and resurrection
    you have set us free;
    you are the Saviour of the world.

4 | The Son of God and his mother

One night my lover was missing from my bed. I got up to look for him but I couldn't find him. I went out into the streets of the city and the roads to seek him, but I searched in vain. The police stopped me and I said to them, "Have you seen him anywhere, the one I love so much?" It was only a little while afterwards that I found him and held him and would not let him go until I had brought him into my mother's old bedroom. I adjure you, O women from Jerusalem, by the gazelles and deer of the park, not to awake my lover. Let him sleep."

SECOND STORY

A WOMAN'S SONG

I had no place in the temples
but the Almighty searched for me
in the underground of my humiliation.
And of me,
condemned to a thousand deaths by all laws,
he built his temple,
without consulting the Teachers of the Law.

The One
from whom I had my origins
asked my permission to become a son of mine.

17

What an enormous and tender weight in my arms
has become the One
who created the Light!

He calls me mother,
and I call him son.
We are inseparable – of the same destiny.
I satisfy his hunger
and clothe his body;
my breast has become a fountain
of sweet and fresh milk for him,
while he floods me
with the delights of his Spirit.
With my hands
I weave his clothes
and his mercy covers my nakedness,
clothing me in joy and exultation...

LET US PRAY

Jesus, help us to reach out beyond
our natural family to become
universal brothers, sisters and
parents, open to those in need of
loving care.

ACCLAMATION

**Lord,
by your cross and resurrection
you have set us free;
you are the Saviour of the world.**

5 | The Son of God needs help

A Jew going on a trip from Jerusalem to Jericho was attacked by bandits. They stripped him of his clothes and money and beat him up and left him half dead beside the road.

But a despised Samaritan came along, and when he saw him he felt deep pity. Kneeling beside him the Samaritan soothed his wounds with medicine and bandaged them. Then he put the man on his donkey and walked along beside him till they came to an inn, where he nursed him through the night. The next day he handed the innkeeper two twenty-pound notes and told him to take care of the man. "If his bills runs higher than that," he said, "I'll pay the difference the next time I am here."

SECOND STORY

GIVE US LIGHT!

One morning I got up,
very sick and dark.
As I opened my window
I prayed, "Give us Light!"

I walked down the street –
people were

frightened, lonely and sad.
I shouted, "Give us Light!"

I learned that
killings, riots and abuses
had been carried out in the night.
I cried, "Give us Light!"

… I wished I could weep
but tears were
dry, deep…
Then in a voiceless yearning
I prayed again, "Give us Light!"

LET US PRAY

Jesus, help us to be recognized as
your own, wherever there are
people suffering from hatred,
conflicts or any kind of injustice.
Give us courage to get involved
even if we have to suffer to bring
about peace and reconciliation.

ACCLAMATION

**Lord,
by your cross and resurrection
you have set us free;
you are the Saviour of the world.**

⑥ The Son of God gives and receives kindness

FIRST STORY
Luke 8:43-48

As they went a woman who wanted to be healed came up behind and touched him, for she had been slowly bleeding for twelve years, and could find no cure (though she had spent everything she had on doctors). But the instant she touched the edge of his robe, the bleeding stopped. "Who touched me?" Jesus asked. Everyone denied it, and Peter said, "Master, so many are crowded against you..." But Jesus told him, "No, it was someone who deliberately touched me, for I felt healing power go out from me." When the woman realized that Jesus knew, she began to tremble and fell to her knees before him and told why she had touched him and that now she was well. "Daughter," he said to her, "your faith has healed you. Go in peace."

SECOND STORY

A WOMAN'S SONG

... Every time
I look for him I find him
in the footpaths, in the fields, in the gardens,
on the mountains, in the houses during meals,
and ignoring the malicious staring eyes
I just pour before him

23

my tears which only he himself gathers.
I offer him my perfume
which only he himself appreciates.
My God rejoices
seeing the gestures of my overflowing love!

Life wells up in my womb
every time his hand touches me.
I exult listening to the words of his lips
and share the anguish of his Spirit...

LET US PRAY

Jesus, we pray for those who care
for the sick, for the lonely and the
dying. Help us to open our hearts
with generosity and without
counting the cost, to give ourselves
to create a world of friendship,
respect and brotherly love.

ACCLAMATION

**Lord,
by your cross and resurrection
you have set us free;
you are the Saviour of the world.**

7 | The Son of God falls a second time

My weary nights are filled with pain as though something were relentlessly gnawing at my bones. All night long I toss and turn, and my garments bind about me. God has thrown me into the mud. I have become as dust and ashes. I cry to you, O God, but you don't answer me. I stand before you and you don't bother to look. You have become cruel towards me, and persecute me with great power and effect. You throw me into the whirlwind and dissolve me in the storm. And I know that your purpose for me is death. I expected my fall to be broken, just as one who falls stretches out his hands or cries for help in his calamity.

And did I not weep for those in trouble? Wasn't I deeply grieved for the needy?

I therefore looked for good to come. Evil came instead. I waited for the light. Darkness came. My heart is troubled and restless. Waves of affliction have come upon me.

SECOND STORY

THE SAPLING

The burning, relentless sun
caused my sapling to dry up,

but the dew gave it a drink
so that my sapling didn't die.
Frost and snow
gave agonies to my sapling,
but a ray of morning light
warmed it up
and the sap
circulated again.
My sapling
had become beautiful!
But, alas!
Again
an insolent insect
gnawed its new-born leaves...
Then
my sapling wept, protested,
but even so
it didn't despair.
When Spring came,
new leaves grew out miraculously.
A violent storm,
bad enough to overthrow cedars,
attacked my sapling
and, with raging jealousy,
started breaking, uprooting,
dragging it a long way off...

Jesus, help us to remember that we have no right to take advantage of our fellow men and women. Give us the courage to defend the weak by standing up to those who oppress them.

ACCLAMATION

**Lord,
by your cross and resurrection
you have set us free;
you are the Saviour of the world.**

The Son of God consoles the women

FIRST STORY
Luke 23:27-31

Great crowds trailed along behind, and many grief-stricken women. But Jesus turned and said to them, "Daughters of Jerusalem, don't weep for me, but for yourselves and for your children. For the days are coming, when the women who have no children will be counted fortunate indeed. Mankind will beg the mountains to fall on them and crush them, and the hills to bury them. For if such things as this are done to me, the Living Tree, what will they do to you?"

SECOND STORY

THE WOMEN

"Women,
don't you weep,
don't you cry!"
God said.

"There are roads
only you can walk,
seeds
only you can plant;

30

Songs
only you can sing,
words
only you can utter;

Hungers
only you can feed,
thirsts
only you can quench.

Women,
don't weep,
don't you cry!"
God said.

"There are joys
only you can give,
pains
only you can bear;

Lives
only you can nourish,
deaths
only you can die;

Secrets
only you can keep,
visions
only you can see.

Therefore,
don't you weep,
don't you cry!"
God said.

"Mothers,
sisters of all
humankind,
you,
mothers and sisters
of mine".

LET US PRAY

Jesus, help us to comfort those who
mourn and weep in our society;
help us not to forget that women
and children are often obliged to
carry a burden too heavy for them,
while their rights are denied to them
and their true worth is not
respected.

ACCLAMATION:

**Lord,
by your cross and resurrection
you have set us free;
you are the Saviour of the world.**

9 | The Son of God falls again

Then I said, O Lord, you deceived me when you promised me your help. I have to give them your message because you are stronger than I am, but now I am the laughing-stock of the city, mocked by all. You have never once let me speak a word of kindness to them; always it is disaster and horror and destruction.

No wonder they scoff and mock and make my name a household joke. And I can't quit! For if I say I'll never again mention the Lord – never more speak in his name– then his word in my heart is like fire that burns in my bones, and I can't hold it any longer. Yet on every side I hear them whispering threats, and I am afraid. "We will report you," they say. Even those who were my friends are watching me, waiting for a fatal slip. "He will trap himself," they say, "and then we will get our revenge on him."

SECOND STORY

EARTHQUAKE IN WINTER

All is dead around me:
in Armenia,
in the railway stations,
everywhere.

34

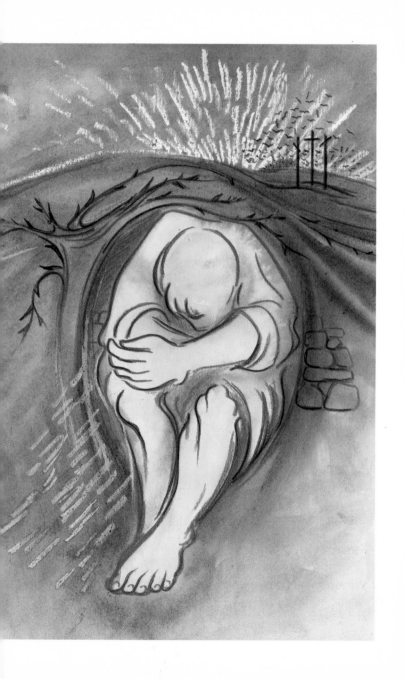

And inside me
all is dead and dark too.
No matter the hour,
the frustrated light
doesn't come through.

The soil
is frozen in the gardens,
people are frozen
under and on the rubble,
all is hard and cold;
under my shoes,
and over my head too.
The fields are barren,
lifeless beings silently cry.

No song can be heard,
the birds are old,
and sit thoughtfully
keeping company to the survivors
around a heatless fire.
Where is the song of lovers?
Where are the colours of life?

I don't understand the secrets of winter,
but I feel its heaviness upon my heart.
My soul is bare,
and my meaningless life
is a miscarriage
of so many hopes...

Jesus, help us to learn from our own sufferings to reach out to the sufferings of others, that instructed by your cross we may become more like you.

ACCLAMATION

**Lord,
by your cross and resurrection
you have set us free;
you are the Saviour of the world.**

10 | The Son of God is exposed naked

FIRST STORY
Philippians 2:5-9

Your attitude should be the kind that was shown us by Jesus Christ, who, though he was God, did not demand and cling to his rights as God, but laid aside his mighty power and glory, taking the disguise of a slave and becoming like men. He humbled himself even further, going so far as actually to die a criminal's death on a cross.

Yet it was because of this that God raised him up to the heights of heaven and gave him a name which is above every other name.

SECOND STORY

FRAGILITY

Someone
clothed in fragility
possesses
neither energies nor resources
in the barns.

Hanging
in the immense emptiness,
he's flogged by the wind
till the marrow of his bones
shows itself in nakedness.

Dancing
in the rain,
he's getting ready to receive
the warmth
of the unimaginable sun.

Pain, frustration, humiliation
dig the deep well
of the hard waters
which flow from the rocky heart of the abyss,
and yet,
they are waters rained down
from the reign of the stars.

What a deep suffering
lies in waiting!
Only fatigue
appears to be the answer
to the desperate hope.

But
everything pushes him forward,
forcing him to draw out
non-existing energy,
while in the desire
everything
assumes the flavour
of last evening's
preparations.

Jesus, help us to be generous like you, not to take as our own what we should always share with other people. Free us from jealousy and greed.

ACCLAMATION:

**Lord,
by your cross and resurrection
you have set us free;
you are the Saviour of the world.**

11 | The Son of God is killed

Matthew 2:16-18

Herod was furious when he learned that the astrologers had disobeyed him. Sending soldiers to Bethlehem, he ordered them to kill every baby boy two years old and under, both in the town and on the nearby farms, for the astrologers had told him the star first appeared to them two years before. This brutal action of Herod's fulfilled the prophecy of Jeremiah,
"Screams of anguish come from Ramah,
weeping unrestrained.
Rachel weeping for her children:
uncomforted –
for they are dead."

SECOND STORY

ABORTION

Life
was sailing in a boat called womb,
while the baby was dreaming
about a beautiful garden
with many many colours
and pools with dancing red fish,
and butterflies jumping from leaf to leaf
and from flower to flower.

There was a cot
in a flower-bed of pure white lace,
with a smiling face hovering over it
singing songs,
and telling many beautiful stories.

One day,
adults sat down
counting the rooms of the flat,
calculating the bank accounts,
measuring the car seats,
and planning the holidays abroad.
"No!" they said,
"We can't afford a cot, can we?"

So
they paid a doctor
to destroy the flowers in the garden,
to kill the dancing fish in the tiny pool.
When the butterflies found no flowers, no leaves
to jump upon,
rubbing their eyes,
uttering a cry of desolation,
they died.

The doctor
threw the cot of lace into the rubbish bin,
and for the first time there were sobbings
to shake the whole world.
No one could sing a song of joy,
no one could remember a story about life.

The earth became void,
the boat sank into darkness

and the hills around
have been sobbing for two thousand years
without stopping.

LET US PRAY

Jesus, forgive us for submitting you
to torture and death, for violating
your human rights. Help us to use
all our talents to give life, not to
destroy it any more.

ACCLAMATION

**Lord,
by your cross and resurrection
you have set us free;
you are the Saviour of the world.**

12 | The Son of God entrusts his mother to us

FIRST STORY
John 19:25-27

Standing near the cross were Jesus' mother, Mary, his aunt, the wife of Cleopas, and Mary Magdalene. When Jesus saw his mother standing there beside me, his close friend, he said to her, "He is your son".

And to me he said, "She is your mother!" And from then on I took her into my home.

SECOND STORY

YOUR VIRGINAL STRENGTH

... Mother,
that fatigue and pain of yours
are gradually transformed
into universal love;
with immense tenderness you go on waiting.

The sufferings of the world
ask to be received
into your virginal womb.
You open yourself to its huge burden
and, fashioning it anew,

you give birth to the sons and daughters
of the New Hope.
Your virginal and serene eyes
are the rocks
against which all despair smashes.

You say,
"Violence will come to an end!"
While embracing
the devastating human pain,
you look towards heaven and pray,
"Wonderful!
The universe is moving in faithfulness and beauty!"

Cold reason
doesn't convince you;
while greeting all misery with tenderness,
you rebuke
all cruelty with firmness.
With your eyes wide open
and your lamp
full of the "oil of joy",
you watch alone.
The night doesn't frighten you;
you know
the Dawn is coming soon!

Jesus, we pray for all mothers whose children are killed by all kinds of violence in our society, and for the children who have no mothers to support them in the struggles of life.

ACCLAMATION

**Lord,
by your cross and resurrection
you have set us free;
you are the Saviour of the world.**

13 | The Son of God draws the world to himself

FIRST STORY
John 12:24-28;31-32

Jesus replied that the time had come for him to return to his glory in heaven, and: "I must fall and die like a kernel of wheat that falls into the furrows of the earth. Unless I die I will be alone – a single seed. But my death will produce many new wheat kernels – a plentiful harvest of new lives. If you love your life down here – you lose it. If you despise your life down here – you will exchange it for eternal glory.

If these Greeks want to be my disciples, tell them to come and follow me, for my servants must be where I am. And if they follow me, the Father will honour them.

Now my soul is troubled. Shall I pray, 'Father' save me from what lies ahead?' But that is the very reason why I came! Father, bring glory and honour to your name...

... The time of judgment for the world has come – and the time when Satan, the prince of this world, shall be cast out. And when I am lifted up (on the cross) I will draw everyone to me."

ON THE MOUNTAIN

Pushed
by the pain of your silence,
I climb the mountain.

On the top,
I meet leaders with lifted arms
until the sun rises.

A cross
is lifted up
against the dark horizon,
from which a fountain flows.
But
it's a fountain
born from a rock beaten by lashes
and pierced by lances.

There are tearless cries,
and I catch a glimpse of a burned land
which starts blooming,
since God himself sent the clouds
to water it.

Then I start loving
your unspoken words,
and your silent steps
like those
of a dancer.

And my dumb verses
dance to the sound
of your silence,
like a field of poppies
in the evening breeze.

LET US PRAY

Jesus, you taught us that unless the
grain of wheat dies, it remains
alone. Give us the courage to
commit our lives to God the Father
so that our existence may turn out to
be a source of joy for everyone we
meet.

ACCLAMATION:

**Lord,
by your cross and resurrection
you have set us free;
you are the Saviour of the world.**

14 | The Son of God is buried

Then a man named Joseph, a member of the Jewish Supreme Court, from the city of Arimathea in Judea, went to Pilate and asked for the body of Jesus. He was a godly man who had been expecting the Messiah's coming and had not agreed with the decision and actions of the other Jewish leaders. So, he took down Jesus' body and wrapped it in a long linen cloth and laid it in a new tomb hewn into the rock (at the side of a hill). This was done on Friday afternoon, the day of preparation for the Sabbath. As the body was taken away, the women from Galilee followed and saw it carried into the tomb. Then they went home and prepared spices and ointments to embalm him; but by the time they were finished it was Sabbath, so they rested all that day as required by the Jewish law.

SECOND STORY

NIGHT

You come to me,
empty of sleep and full of ghosts.

In you,
there is no rest for pilgrim feet,
nor solace for tormented spirits.

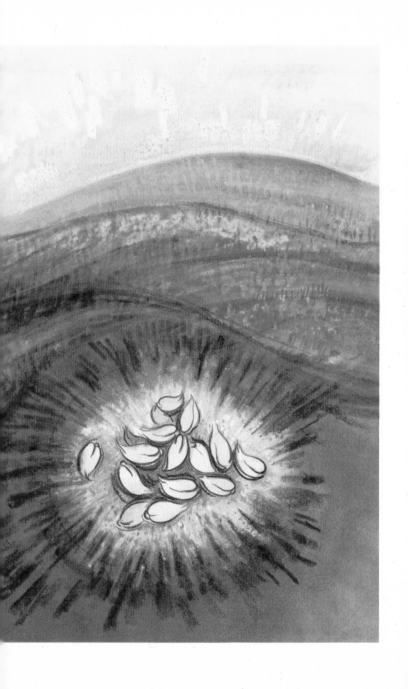

To my pain,
you answer painless,
"There's no room!"

Night, blind night,
time will come
when the Light
will be born from you.

Night, old night,
worn out with silence and waiting,
now
you hold me prisoner in darkness
but one day
I'll be enlightened by the young Dawn.

Night, deaf night,
I'll call you with a new name
when you lead me to the Day.

LET US PRAY

Jesus, give us strength to endure our
daily frustrations and sufferings,
believing that you give meaning
even to our own death.

ACCLAMATION

**Lord,
by your cross and resurrection
you have set us free;
you are the Saviour of the world.**

15 | The Son of God is risen

FIRST STORY:
John 20:1-9

Early Sunday morning, while it was still dark, Mary Magdalene came to the tomb and found that the stone was rolled aside from the entrance.

She ran and found Simon Peter and me and said, "They have taken the Lord's body away out of the tomb, and I don't know where they have put him!"

We ran to the tomb to see: I outran Peter and got there first, and stooped and looked in and saw the linen cloth lying there but I did not go in. Then Simon Peter arrived and went on inside. He also noticed the cloth lying there while the swathe that had covered Jesus' head was rolled up in a bundle and was lying at the side. Then I went in too, and saw, and believed (that he had risen) for until then we hadn't realized that the Scripture said he would come to life again!

SECOND STORY

A WOMAN'S SONG

... They tried to convince me that
"Mary's son" was possessed, a fanatic, a rebel
against the laws of the Most High,
and they punished him,
nailing him to a cross!...

I died with him believing in his life,
and embraced his dead body to my body;
the body of my son
made of my own flesh and blood...!
... I kissed his wounds
with tenderness and compassion.
They had hidden him from my eyes
in a dark tomb behind an enormous stone
but I was there hiding in the night myself,
comforting him with my kisses,
washing him with my tears,
embalming him with my perfumes.
When the "strong" and the "wise"
had fallen asleep, I was awake,
and then I heard his voice calling me again.
"Woman! Mother! Sister! Mary!
Go! Tell my brothers I am alive!!!"

I answered, "My Lord and God!
Son! Brother! Rabbi!
All my being tells of you.
He is risen! He lives for ever!
Alleluia!!!"

LET US PRAY

> Jesus, give us the joyful hope of
> living with you for ever.

ACCLAMATION

> **Lord,**
> **by your cross and resurrection**
> **you have set us free;**
> **you are the Saviour of the world.**

Resurrection:
Three days' walk
from the cross

If you forgive Christ
for letting himself be nailed on the cross;

If you have learned from the crucified One
to forgive those
who despise and hurt you;

If you pray harder
when anguish and affliction
are heavy upon you;

If you work with all your strength
to achieve justice,
setting people free from greed and misery;

If you never give up in the face of despair,
believing that God is Life;

If you look for God
in the midst of people
and where nature grows;

If you live life to the full,
knowing for certain that the resurrection
abides just a three days' walk
from the foot of the cross;

Then you've already met
the Living One.
Alleluia!

CONCLUSION

We come to the end of the Way of the Cross with
a feeling that all is accomplished, and yet that the
whole process is to continue. The Son of God,
Jesus, has completed his mission in obedience.
Through this he showed us the depth of God's
love. Nevertheless, you and me, who are the sons
and daughters of God, find ourselves in the growth
process, still striving to become perfect in love like
him.

But after Christ's resurrection we are no longer
in total darkness, for the first-born Son became the
Way leading us to victory over sin and death.

"By his wounds we have been healed."

Comboni and the Cross

Christ crucified was the main strength and guide of Bishop Daniel Comboni (1831-1881), founder of the Comboni Missionaries. He knew that through the Cross God's wisdom was at work in every human situation. When disappointment, fatigue, loneliness, sickness and death came his way he believed more than ever that victory was just round the corner. And so he surrendered in hope to the mystery of a God who died on the Cross for the salvation of all humankind — and so for the salvation of his beloved Africa too.

As a disciple of the Son of God, Comboni willingly paid the price of love. His premature death brought the seed of life to the fertile ground of the many African calvaries. When he realized that his earthly life was coming to an end, he asked his friends not to give up and to bear in mind that God's works are born at the foot of the Cross.

The four thousand women and men born from his passionate love for the poorest and most abandoned of the earth keep their eyes fixed on the Crucified One as he lives in today's world and serve him there.

In the UK and Ireland the Comboni Missionaries run Vocation Centres staffed with missionaries who have the experience and the time to help you think about becoming part of the Church's worldwide mission. Why not get in touch?

Please write or ring any of these addresses:

Ireland:
Comboni Mission Centre, 29 Woodfarm Avenue,
Palmerstown, Dublin 20. Tel.: 265951

Scotland:
Comboni Missionaries, 151 Baillieston Road, Shettleston,
Glasgow G32 0TN. Tel.: 041-771 5242
Comboni Missionary Sisters, 124 Berryknowes Road,
Cardonald, Glasgow G52 2TT. Tel.: 041-883 6139

England:
Comboni Missionaries, Brownberrie Lane, Horsforth,
Leeds LS18 5HE. Tel.: (0532) 582658
Comboni Missionary Sisters, 4 Chiswick Lane, London W4 2JF.
Tel.: 081-994 0449

The Comboni Family

Sister Carmen's "Missionary Way of the Cross" has led you in prayer to encounter Jesus Crucified as he continues to bear his Cross together with his suffering brothers and sisters throughout the world today. The Comboni missionary family exists to serve the poorest and most abandoned, those who are deprived both of basic human rights and of the knowledge of Jesus. We would like to invite you to join this family and here are some of the ways you can do this:

1. Through your prayers: we need this support in all aspects of our work. Especially we need you to join us in asking the Lord of the Harvest to send labourers into his harvest.

2. By keeping in touch through our magazine COMBONI MISSIONS. All those who send a minimum donation of £5 to one of the Missions Offices (addresses below) will receive the magazine regularly, together with a Newsletter and a free copy of our calendar.

3. By sending a donation from time to time or by making a covenant to increase the value of your donation without any extra cost to yourself. Given certain conditions the Inland Revenue will give us the tax you have paid on the amount you give to the missions. Details from any of the addresses below.

4. By joining the Holy Redeemer Guild as a way of sharing in the prayers and apostolate of the Comboni Missionaries worldwide.

5. By remembering us in your will.

For further information please contact the Director of Missionary Activities at any of these addresses:

Comboni Missionaries, London Road, Sunningdale, Berkshire SL5 0JX. Tel.: (0990) 21267

Comboni Missionaries, 151 Baillieston Road, Shettleston, Glasgow G32 0TN. Tel.: 041-771 5242

Comboni Missionary Sisters, 4 Chiswick Lane, London W4 2JF. Tel.: 081-994 0449

Comboni Missionaries, 29 Woodfarm Avenue, Palmerstown, Dublin 20. Tel.: 265951

Praying with Comboni

If you have enjoyed praying with Comboni Missionaries in this booklet, perhaps you would like to know about some other missionary publications. They will help you to grow in your sense of belonging to the Comboni family throughout the world and they will especially help to make your prayer more missionary and aware of the needs of the poorest and most abandoned. The publications featured here are all available from the addresses on the previous page.

A HEART FOR AFRICA tells the stirring missionary story of Bishop Daniel Comboni, first bishop of Central Africa. Through the events of his vocation and ministry we are helped to reflect on our own journey of discipleship and to discover the different ways in which the Lord is leading us into mission today. Author Bernard Ward was a missionary in Malawi and presently is working in South Africa.

Daniel Comboni left his missionaries a great love for the Heart of Jesus as the source of missionary enthusiasm and fire. In NO GREATER LOVE we offer a missionary novena to the Heart of Jesus, nine days of prayer based on the Scriptures to deepen and enrich our devotion to the Sacred Heart, opening it up to the presence of the Crucified Christ in today's world.

THE MISSIONARY ROSARY is a new, fresh way of praying with an ancient formula. At each decade there are scripture passages and a short prayer together with a suggestion to pray for one of the five continents. In this way we draw close to Mary in order to open our hearts and minds to the whole world.

Ed Stobart

Alan Millar

Ian Allan PUBLISHING

CONTENTS

First published 2001

ISBN 0 7110 2640 8

Published by Ian Allan Publishing

an imprint of Ian Allan Publishing Ltd, Hersham, Surrey KT12 4RG.
Printed by Ian Allan Printing Ltd, Hersham, Surrey KT12 4RG.

Code: 0301/D

Front cover: MAN F2000 H1671 (W671 PAO) *Candy.* **Alan Millar**

Back cover : A line-up of Volvo FL10s. **Mike Greenwood**

Title page: Livery detail on the company's preserved Atkinson (see page 33), showing the initials of Edward Pears Stobart, the original Eddie Stobart, and father of the founder of the modern haulage business who prefers to be known as Edward. **Mike Greenwood**

Above: H171 (M171 THH), a two-axle Scania R113M tractor unit and three-axle curtain-sided semi-trailer at a service area on the M1. *Emilia Victoria* has a 360hp Scania 11-litre engine. ***Alan Millar***

Left: The 'S' chevrons, the diagonally-striped bumpers and the girl's name all identify MAN F2000 tractor unit H1596 (T596 JHH) as an Eddie Stobart truck. In recent years, increasing numbers of German-built MANs have been added to the fleet in its quest to run the most cost-effective vehicles it can find. ***Alan Millar***

INTRODUCTION

Eddie Stobart has become a British institution. The loveable face of road haulage. This is no small achievement — on several counts. The public hasn't always liked the truck, lorry, wagon or juggernaut — call it what you will, and many have called it worse — for it's seen as a large, noisy, intrusive, intimidating and polluting vehicle that's usually delivering someone else's goods. The image of the driver used to be no better, seen as an unwashed, unhealthy, uncultured brute behind the wheel of a vehicle with similarly negative characteristics.

That stereotype usually grew up in complete ignorance. The perception was reinforced by television comedy and by the lack of opportunity for ordinary people to meet the real truck drivers, who often are among the most intelligent, articulate, considerate and highly professional men and women you could ever hope to meet on a road journey. It also grew up as the road freight transport industry appeared incapable of cultivating a better public image for itself.

Then along came Eddie Stobart. The first 15 years of this haulage business's existence, from launch in 1970 until it embarked on a rapid growth plan from around 1985, were spent in relative obscurity. There weren't enough of its smart green, white, red and gold trucks around for many people to notice them. But when the business grew, something captured the public's imagination.

It was partly the name. Few people are likely ever to have known anyone called Stobart. It's not one of Britain's most

Above: A row of Volvo FL10 tractor units lined up and ready for action on the motorway network in June 1996. Nearest the camera is H626 (M626 TAO), named *Audrey*. The trucks nearest it are named *Katey*, *Philippa* and *Amanda*. **Mike Greenwood**

common surnames. But it's short enough to be memorable and when it's linked to a friendly-sounding abbreviated forename like Eddie, it's even more memorable. There was little chance of not noticing it on the motorways when it was displayed in the largest lettering possible on the sides of the company's rapidly-growing fleet of curtain-sided trailer vans. Certainly, all that attracted the musician Jools Holland who mentioned the trucks in an interview that sparked off some BBC disc jockeys into encouraging listeners to notice Eddie Stobart trucks on their journeys. But there was something else. Three other somethings, in fact.

The trucks were always clean and smartly painted. The drivers were kitted out in a clean uniform with a collar and clip-on tie at a time when the industry's standard uniform was a pair of jeans and a dirty tee-shirt or a one-size-fits-all boiler suit. And the trucks all had girls' names.

Lots of other trucks had names, too, but the novelty of identifying the names on smart-looking trucks controlled by smart-looking drivers added a finishing touch to an image transformation other businesses would have spent billions trying to achieve. Without necessarily trying to do as much, this Carlisle company helped make people see trucks as something positive, a boon rather than a threat. The cult of 'Eddie spotting' became a national sport somehow more socially acceptable than train spotting.

The adulation didn't stop there. Such has been the volume of fan mail that has poured into Eddie Stobart Ltd over the past 12 years that the company was prompted to establish a fan club that spawned a whole sub-economy of merchandising sales — of

Above: Another 1996 line-up, but this time of Leyland DAF 95 drawbar units. Nearest the camera is M386 (J49 XHH), named *Janette*. The Chep pallets beyond the trucks play an essential part in carrying the loads aboard the company's trucks. ***Mike Greenwood***

Above: A Volvo FH12 on one of the motorway trunk runs that characterise the Eddie Stobart operation. *Garry Donnelly*

Right: A Leyland DAF 95 curtain-sider and drawbar trailer on the M1 in Buckinghamshire. *Alan Millar*

memorabilia from teddy bears to tea bags, truck models to children's toys, story books and clothing.

The Eddie Stobart story isn't just about fan clubs, teddy bears and tea bags. It's about how one business has developed a ruthlessly customer-focused approach to meeting the transport and distribution requirements of the new British economy.

How it selects and motivates its drivers and maintains an image others would pay millions to try and cultivate. In short, how one company — and one man behind its growth — has changed the face of British road haulage and is now going on to compete in mainland Europe.

This book sets out to tell a little more of the Stobart story, of its development from modest beginnings to become the largest privately-owned truck operator in Britain. It looks at the makes and models of trucks it operates and at what determines its choice of vehicles, at how its distinctive livery came into being and at how its network has grown and is beginning to take the company increasingly across Europe.

It isn't in any way an official company history, but it couldn't have been written without the company's co-operation. I'm especially grateful to Edward Stobart — the unassuming brains behind this highly successful enterprise — for spending time explaining how the company ticks and how it has developed, and my thanks also to William Stobart, Commercial Director Barrie Thomas and to Deborah Rodgers for setting up the meetings with all three.

If you have any specific comments or questions about the contents of this book, please contact the publisher, Ian Allan Publishing, at Riverdene Business Park, Molesey Road, Hersham, Surrey, KT12 4RG. Don't trouble Eddie Stobart staff who work very hard running and developing a successful road haulage and distribution company.

If you wish to join the Eddie Stobart Fan Club and receive regular details of such facts as the identity of its regularly changing fleet, its address is Brunthill Road, Kingstown Industrial Estate, Carlisle, Cumbria, CA3 0EH. Alternatively, log on to the company's website at www.eddiestobart.co.uk.

Alan Millar
Glasgow
February 2001

1. THIRTY YEARS OF GROWTH - THE STOBART STORY SO FAR

Above: *Josaphine*, Iveco Ford Cargo F373 (H477 VHH), was a rigid local-delivery truck with a curtain-sided body and sleeper cab. This Cargo model was introduced in 1981 as a Ford, and production ended in 1992, six years after Iveco acquired control of Ford's European truck business in a joint venture. This was among the last of this style of Cargo to be built before Iveco's replacement EuroCargo completely replaced the range.
Garry Donnelly

As in the best tales of business success, Eddie Stobart — Britain's best-known road haulier and the one with the biggest and maybe even the only fan club in the country (if not the world) — has risen from modest beginnings. Indeed, for its first 15 years this company showed no more obvious promise of great growth than the hundreds and thousands of small operators which came or went in the 1970s.

On 23 November 1970, when Eddie Stobart Ltd was founded as a limited

company, Edward Stobart — second son of the man whose name is as common a sight on our motorways today as the words 'Next Services' or 'Watch your speed' — was still a 14-year-old who helped out in the family firm. His father's business bought and sold agricultural fertilisers and was contracted to spread them on farmers' fields around Cumberland. It needed a small lorry fleet to collect fertiliser from manufacturers and deliver it to farms, and subcontracted a lot of this work to smaller haulage contractors.

Below: Another Stobart revolution was to make widespread use of drawbar combinations. Their ability to maximise load space, as shown here by Volvo F10 M378 (J351 XAO) *Eileen Anne*, has been reduced by the advent of longer trailers on more conventional articulated vehicles. *Garry Donnelly*

When Edward became involved in running the transport operation in 1975, it still had only six vehicles, but this was enough for him to begin putting into practice the dynamic business methods that have driven it up to a 1,000-vehicle operation today. He worked a 20-hour day then, in the office by day and driving lorries by night. Another secret of those first steps to extraordinary success was to find loads to fill the fertiliser lorries on empty outward legs of collection runs and similarly empty return legs of delivery runs.

Before long, the company was picking up two-way loads and the transport operation began to build up a momentum of its own. It made sense to split the business in two, with Eddie Stobart (Trading) Ltd becoming the

agricultural company with a dedicated lorry fleet of its own, while Eddie Stobart Ltd concentrated on developing its transport expertise. In 1977, by which time the fleet had doubled to the then dizzy heights of 12 vehicles, it moved from Caldbeck in the Cumbrian countryside into rented premises in Carlisle's Greystone Road.

It was then — having won some work from the Metal Box Company to deliver empty beer cans to breweries — that the company also took the brave decision to invest in curtain-sided trailers. Until the late 1970s, most haulage companies followed the traditional practice of roping and sheeting loads on open, flatbed trailers. Besides the fact that this was how loads had been secured since the birth of motorised road

Above: Petra Anne, a Seddon Atkinson 3-11 tractor unit retained for use as a yard shunter. This model was part of a series of trucks produced by Oldham-based Seddon Atkinson between 1975 and 1992, during which time the manufacturer went through periods of American and Spanish ownership before becoming part of Iveco.
Garry Donnelly

freight (and before that, too), the one great virtue of roping and sheeting was the low cost of buying such simple trailers; but Edward Stobart had seen how own-account operators — companies like his father's which ran lorries simply to move their own goods — were deriving real benefits from running these more expensive, new-fangled curtain-sided bodies. At the time, he says, curtain-siders were about twice as expensive to buy as flatbeds, but they took far less time to make ready for the road than a laboriously tethered flatbed; also the load was waterproofed and there was less risk of damage in transit. Here was an opportunity to invest in equipment which would give the

company a clear advantage over the great mass of general hauliers selling their services to British industry. With characteristic astuteness, he also built on that early Metal Box cans contract to secure return traffic by carrying full cans from the brewers. Food and beverages today account for around 90% of the company's business, helping make Eddie Stobart Britain's largest haulier of soft drinks.

Another vital peg for the future was driven into the Cumbrian soil in 1980 when the company seized the chance to move onto part of the Kingstown Trading Estate in Carlisle, the hub of its operations today, and a site within exceptionally easy reach of the

M6. It still only had 25 vehicles at this point. Over the 20 years since then, it has taken advantage of the availability of additional land for acquisition and occupies about 30 acres — 20% of the whole estate — with several truck manufacturers' dealers as near neighbours. Its first plot of land at Kingstown showed the company's astute approach to business; it was offered land near the front of the estate, but preferred to take a cheaper site at the back and exercise the option of expanding as the business grew.

A DIFFERENT STANDARD OF SERVICE

Having seized one advantage over its competition by investing in curtain-siders, Eddie Stobart also began to stand apart from its competitors by offering a different standard of service. It provided same-day and next-day deliveries from one end of the country to the other, using smartly-presented vehicles driven by equally smart, uniformed drivers. As Edward Stobart says, this wasn't a question of cleaning up the company's act; it set out to be clean from Day One.

Presentation was part of an aim to bend over backwards to meet its customers' needs. In haulage, as in many other areas of business, there often is a gulf between operators' willingness to pay lip service to the idea that 'the customer is king' or 'the customer is always right' and the reality of the service it provides, but for Eddie Stobart Ltd, the path to growth was paved by a determination to do as bidden by its customers. It's a policy that owes a lot to the business's modest beginnings and huge ambitions.

Below: A later Seddon Atkinson, Strato 325 tractor unit H012 (F287 FHH), named *Sadie*. The Strato was produced between 1988 and 1992 and used the Cabtec cab developed jointly by Seddon Atkinson's then Spanish parent company, ENASA (which also made Pegaso trucks in Spain) and DAF. The cab was bought in far greater numbers on Stobart's fleet of DAF 95s and 95XFs. *Mike Greenwood*

Above: Three yard shunters are nearest the camera in this view, with, from left to right, Seddon Atkinson *Petra Anne* numbered SHUNT 12, Ford Cargo *Anita* numbered SHUNT 08 and an ERF B-Series. ***Mike Greenwood***

It learned very quickly that it was just another small haulier in the big distribution worlds of the companies for which it worked in the 1970s and early 1980s. Edward Stobart says the policy today, just as it was then, is not to pass his company's problems on to his customers. 'We never raise a complaint if the customer wants a load taken over a long distance over a weekend,' he says. Now that may seem self-evident today, but, as he recalls, the transport world of 25 years ago was different; manufacturers had to ask hauliers how many deliveries could be made on each day of the week and then geared their production around the transport service they could buy. In his view, that was a back-to-front arrangement. He resolved to redefine the road-haulage business, to respond to industry's needs and offer clients positive solutions rather than present them with problems and reasons why their goods

could not be delivered. In short, the Stobart philosophy was to be a 'no-problem haulier'. The idea, which began to gain momentum as word got around, was that customers would begin to put more work onto Stobart vehicles when they experienced the difference in service.

It wasn't an overnight revolution. Bigger, longer-established operators defended their businesses by taking on all of some businesses' traffic when the economy was quieter, and this Cumbrian newcomer had to work away at eroding the long-standing relationships which existed between many customers and hauliers. Added to that, in an age when profit margins across industry were greater than today, the haulage budget was accepted as a sum of money which had to be paid. Many manufacturers and wholesalers never questioned it. Today, thanks in part to Eddie Stobart Ltd, there often is no budget for haulage; industry expects its transport to be provided as cheaply and efficiently as possible.

Eddie Stobart Ltd has survived and, indeed, thrived in this cut-throat world by keeping its cost base down. In the jargon of today, it is lean, mean and hungry for work. Edward Stobart still works a full week and believes this sets the tone for the way the rest of the business should function. 'We're not paying a lot of retired people. We are a very young company, which is important. We're still very slick and we've not forgotten our grass roots. We don't allow our senior management to forget what it was like in the beginning to get loads and contracts; we've got to keep going to prevent others from getting our work,' he says.

The company refuses to stand still, seeing itself as a competitor in an arduous athletics event. 'We're going over hurdles each year, and when we get to a "safe" position we find another hurdle,' says Edward Stobart. 'We're never satisfied and secure. In fact, we still feel very insecure as a business. We've got to keep going forward and jumping over those hurdles; that's the only secure thing we can do, because if we sit back, we will go backwards faster than we grew up.'

THE STRATEGIC DEPOT APPROACH

Going forwards has been achieved partly by developing a strategic depot network which, in turn, has created the foundation of a national express-delivery service. The process began in 1986 when a depot was opened at Burnaston airfield, near Burton-upon-Trent; today, Toyota's main European car factory is at Burnaston, but Eddie Stobart Ltd got there first because one of its customers needed to have a warehouse within easy reach of a key customer which required just-in-time deliveries. This fitted into Stobart's expansion plans because it wanted to start basing some of its vehicles in the Midlands, so it could deliver goods between Carlisle and the Midlands in one shift and similarly between the Midlands and London in a shift. By 1989, the depot network had been expanded to include sites in Stamford, Knottingley and Glasgow, and the Burnaston operation was moved to another site in Burton itself.

Each depot is different. Some are purely transport depots, with parking for trucks and trailers and little else, some are purely for warehousing, while others combine both functions. Some sites have vehicle-maintenance and washing facilities and some of the warehouses have high-bay racking systems to accommodate larger quantities of goods. The layout of each depends on individual customers' needs; it isn't dictated by Eddie Stobart Ltd.

They do, however, have one major factor in common: each is on a major road network, with the largest depots no more than one to two miles from a key motorway link. That, as Edward Stobart points out, is for a fundamental reason. 'It's because miles are money. If a vehicle has to go 10 miles off route, that is dead money that you can't get back.' So, he says, the company is prepared to pay good prices for the best-located sites. 'We often have to pay more for land for the best locations, but that pays off in the end . . . even if the bank manager doesn't always agree.'

Because it has such a network, Stobart is able to deploy a significant proportion of its fleet on depot-to-depot trunk runs — an arrangement that improves the reliability of the delivery service it offers to industry. 'It means that if you're held up on motorways and a driver cannot get to his intended destination, he can drive legally to the nearest depot and have the delivery completed from there,' explains Edward Stobart. The point of legality is important, for less-well-resourced haulage firms may place their drivers in the impossible position of having to decide either

Below: Ford Cargo yard shunter *Anita* with a tri-axle curtain-sided trailer. Cargo tractor units were more common before the tie-up with Iveco, which already produced a more comprehensive range of heavier trucks. After Iveco ceased producing the Cargo in Europe, production transferred to Ashok Leyland in India, a company in which Iveco is a major shareholder; Ford also fitted the Cargo cab to trucks sold in the Americas.
Mike Greenwood

to abandon an urgently-required delivery or else break the legal driving and working hours limits if they find themselves being delayed by congestion, accidents or bad weather.

The Stobart depots are never more than 100 miles apart on major trunk routes, and sometimes as close as 50 miles. Glasgow is the farthest north, Poole the farthest south. There also are depots at Bridgwater and Sittingbourne. Deliveries north of Glasgow can be completed within a single shift.

THE VITALLY-IMPORTANT UNIFORMED DRIVERS

While the depots form the backbone of the Stobart network and the service it is able to provide, they could not function without the driving staff. As in any transport business,

these employees are often the only representatives of the company that customers — or customers' customers — meet on a regular basis. The impression they create by their appearance and manner will play a huge part in forming an opinion of how the company functions and whether customers want to continue placing their business with it. So from an early stage, Eddie Stobart Ltd recognised the importance of recruiting the right people to work for it, looking after them properly and kitting them out in smart uniforms rather than leaving them to wear casual clothes or dirty overalls.

When uniforms were first introduced in the late 1980s, the drivers came in for a fair degree of stick from other companies' drivers. 'When we first put drivers into collars and ties, the hassle they got from other drivers was dreadful,' Edward Stobart recalled in an interview given in 1994 . 'They would go into a transport café and be laughed at.' Today, the tables have been turned and it has become the norm, at least with leading haulage companies, to provide their drivers with a similar standard of uniforms. In a later interview with *FHM* magazine — the interest of a mass-market lads' magazine shows just how high-profile the Stobart fleet has become — he said: 'It was also about the same time that we started getting loads of fan mail, almost all of it congratulating the drivers on their appearance and thanking us for making the haulage industry smarter.'

It's a sackable offence not to wear the uniform to the required standard, and it's made easy by supplying clip-on ties. As the boss spelt it out in that same *FHM* interview: 'If one of the drivers comes swanning in without their tie and with three buttons undone, complaining that it's too hot, then they will get told to leave. That's them sacking themselves rather than me deciding to get rid of them.' Haircuts aren't compulsory, but the company's concern for good appearance has seen it install a barber's shop in its new depot at Crick, Northamptonshire.

It's no exaggeration to say that a Stobart driver is more often than not a personable, well-motivated individual as far removed as you can get from the worst stereotypes of the lorry driver. The process of selecting the right people is a well-practised and well-executed one. Whether it's looking for drivers, secretarial support, warehouse staff or cleaners, the approach is the same. 'We look for attitude,' says Edward Stobart. 'If they've not got the right attitude, then it doesn't matter how many degrees they've got. It's an attitude to life in general that we're talking about. Our policy is that if you're not going to enjoy yourself at work, if you're miserable at work, then don't come

into the business at any level.

'We need to have happy people because they will work better. The way to create happy people is to treat them right. That's not just about how much you pay them, but how you speak to them.' It's an approach that, he says, is more like a partnership between the company and motivated employees. 'We look for people who will be quick learners, who can come into our business. It's down to them and us to find the right slot in the company.'

Experience has taught the Stobart company that it will grow most successfully by developing the right people to take it forward. Around 95% of the senior management and directors have been recruited from within, starting at the sharp end and progressing rapidly as the company itself has got bigger. For instance, most contract managers — the people responsible for day-to-day contact with regular customers — as well as traffic office staff all began as drivers, so they know what one of today's drivers is experiencing out on busy motorways or waiting to collect or deliver from industrial premises. The company believes it would have been disastrous had it opted instead to bring people in from outside companies and try and make them fit in with a well-established company culture. It's happy to take a mix of people — those who are satisfied and happy performing routine operational tasks and others who want to grow with the business. 'It's important for us to pick people who are able to take a number of steps at a time,' says Edward Stobart. And just as drivers wear a uniform, so do its other staff. Green sweaters, blazers and ties are order of the working day, blouses and summer skirts for women, pinafores for catering staff in the company restaurants where managers and employees eat together. There's even a company fabric pattern, incorporating the chevron logo from truck cabs, and it's called Edwina — the feminine equivalent of Edward or Eddie.

WHAT MIGHT THE FUTURE HOLD?

Eddie Stobart today is the largest privately-owned truck operator in the UK and one of the 10 biggest in Europe. It has grown at an average rate of 26% per year for the past 10 years and has similar expectations of future growth. It wants to remain privately owned — the only shareholders are Edward, with 55% of the company, and his younger brother William, with 45% — as it doesn't want to have its strategy dictated by City investors' needs.

For now, its business is all undertaken by road, but the company doesn't limit its horizon to trucks in the future. 'One day, sooner rather than later, we hope that we will also be operating on rail,' says the boss. 'A lot of extra haulage in future might be by rail.' Already, the business has hedged its bets on a multi-modal future by having a major presence on the rail-connected Crick development in Northamptonshire, close to the M1/M6/A14 intersection. Longer-term, if the conditions allow it, the company would like to be able to run its own trains along the upgraded West Coast main line. It has already undertaken some research into the possibilities of running its own rail freight business — there is a division ready for action by the name of Eddie Stobart Rail — and it has been tantalising the market with a fanciful painting showing a Stobart-liveried Class 37 diesel locomotive hauling freight wagons alongside the M6 near Tebay. One day, similar sights — presumably with a newer generation of trains — might become reality.

The company has also been an inspiration for others whose liveries and use of curtain-sided trailers owes a lot to Stobart practice. A notable example is James Irlam & Sons of Chelford, Cheshire, which has similar standards to those of Eddie Stobart, and models of whose trucks are sold in the Stobart shop. Indeed, the red, white and gold Irlam trucks work alongside Stobart's green, red, white and gold ones on a Britvic and Coca-Cola drinks contract shared on a 50/50 basis between the two. The client's original plan had been to place the work with one haulier, but it needed the flexibility of two to handle high and sometimes sudden seasonal demand for its products; instead, it treats the two businesses as if they were one and would regard an operational failure by one of the operators as a joint one.

The Eddie Stobart company believes it has already played a pivotal part in ensuring that Britain still has its own road-haulage industry and that our roads haven't been swamped entirely by the vehicles of mainland European rivals. 'If we'd not got where we are, there would be far more vehicles around from fleets like Willi Betz and Norbert Dentressangle. We're seen as the Big Daddy now.' Not bad for a company that only had six vehicles back in 1975, but it may have to endure some short-term pain. In December 2000, the *Sunday Times* reported that rising fuel costs had led to its first-ever trading loss, and that a restructure would lead to 150 redundancies. Previously, it had a 3% profit margin and those losses were confined to the core UK trucking business, which accounted for 55% of sales. The company fully expects to return to profitability.

2. THE FUSSY APPROACH TO BUYING THE RIGHT TRUCKS

Above: MAN F2000 H599 (T599 JHH) *Leah Sinead* in the yard at the Carlisle headquarters. The curtains are held in place by the straps along the bottom of the trailer body. The same name was carried before by two Iveco EuroTech tractors, H612 (M612 SAO) and H367 (P367 CRM). ***Alan Millar***

The Eddie Stobart method of purchasing vehicles is as thorough and well researched as all other key parts of the business.

As Edward Stobart explains, the approach is simple. 'We're very fussy about the trucks that we buy. We aren't truck enthusiasts. What we are, are business people moving goods from A to B and it's important that we purchase the right vehicle to do each job.' Experience has taught the company to look at several factors when buying its trucks, the most important of which are the capital cost of the vehicle and its running costs. The decision on which truck is bought is likely to be a balance between those two. Sometimes a truck that's cheaper to buy may have far higher operating costs, either because it uses more fuel or requires more expensive replacement parts, so it makes good business sense to pay more for a vehicle which will cost less to run over the period of ownership.

The same applies to the rate at which the truck will depreciate over the period it works for the Stobart fleet. 'It's the value of the vehicle after three years that is important, so we get the right price for it when we're finished with it,' he explains. So just as a more expensive vehicle might sometimes cost less to run, it's possible that the more expensive option may also cost less in depreciation while it's in the fleet.

In recent years, spiralling diesel prices have made fuel consumption one of the most important factors — perhaps *the* most important factor — to consider when buying new trucks. 'Twenty or thirty years ago, it used to be reliability. But we can rule that out of the equation today. Every make of truck on the market is very good. There is a very slight margin between the worst and the best. Now we look at the purchase price, the buy-back price [what the manufacturer or its dealer commits itself to paying to take it back after three years] and at fuel consumption,' says Edward Stobart.

When it placed its first volume order for Mercedes-Benz trucks — 20 1834LS tractor units in 1996 on a two-year contract-hire deal for working out of Warrington depot — he made no bones about why he hadn't bought many before. 'We have run the odd Mercedes in the past and they have always proved to be reliable, quality vehicles. But there are a lot of other excellent trucks on the market too. Unfortunately, we have previously found that Mercedes vehicles also carried a premium price tag which we were

Below: After years of feeling that Mercedes-Benz trucks were too expensive for volume purchases, Stobart's began taking them in larger quantities from 1996. H579 (M579 RHH) named *Deborah* was an 1834LS. The 20 supplied in 1996 came in a contract-hire deal with Mercedes subsidiary CharterWay and were supplied by the manufacturer's Carlisle dealer. *Mike Greenwood*

Above: ERF EC10 H528 (L528 MHH) stands next to a preserved Southampton Corporation Guy Arab III double-deck bus. *Mike Greenwood*

19

Above: A Volvo FL10 and a Renault Major pause between journeys. *Mike Greenwood*

Below: H537 (L537 MHH) *Mary Emma*, a since-sold ERF EC10. *Garry Donnelly*

Above: A 1996 line-up with seven Cabtec-cabbed trucks, three ERF EC10s and a Volvo FL10. Four of the Cabtec trucks are DAF 95s, including H081 (J740 XHH) *Catriona* nearest the camera, while the other three — including H426 (K426 DAO) *Heather Emma-Jane*, second from the left — are Seddon Atkinson Stratos.
Mike Greenwood

not prepared to pay. However, I am pleased to see that this is changing and that today Mercedes vehicles appear to be very much more competitively priced than was once the case.'

Even before the mass protests and blockades of September 2000 brought the issue completely into the public domain, fuel consumption was a well-measured cause for concern at the Eddie Stobart business — an issue determining more and more which types of vehicle it would buy. One tenth of a mile per gallon in fuel consumption is worth £200,000 a year across the whole fleet; a mile per gallon is worth £2 million. 'If we can achieve 8.8mpg rather than 8.7mpg, that's £200,000 off the bottom line and often it's easier to put a system in that will save us £100,000 a year rather than find one that will earn ourselves another £100,000,' says the boss.

Knowing that sort of thing has taught the Stobart business to be ruthless with under-

performing vehicles. 'We've always had the attitude that we should not put up with one bad truck. The first loss is the best loss; if we can get rid of something — or someone for that matter — that's doing us no favours, then that's the best thing to do. We should get rid of it no matter what it costs at that time.'

One such lesson was not to buy secondhand trucks. Back in the late 1970s, when the company was just beginning to grow, it bought a few and had them refurbished. It's something many companies still do today, and indeed the buy-back prices for Stobart's three-year-old vehicles are underpinned by the knowledge that they will find ready buyers. But it didn't work for Stobart's in the late 1970s, and it's bought new ever since. It prefers not to inherit someone else's problems with a discarded vehicle and finds that, while the annual depreciation write-off sums for a five-year-old truck are little different from those for a

Above: A once-common type now phased out of Stobart service is the Volvo F10, built between 1977 and 1995. J351 XAO *Eileen Anne* was a drawbar outfit. ***Mike Greenwood***

Below: A wintry view of Seddon Atkinson Strato tractor unit K453 DAO *Kirsten*. ***Garry Donnelly***

new truck's first year, the operating costs are higher. It's likely to require more expensive repairs and will lack the benefits of newer technology, so it may be less fuel-efficient, might wear out tyres more quickly and be less comfortable for drivers to work in.

So whether it purchases them outright, opts for contract hire or leasing deals, Eddie Stobart Ltd sources new vehicles. The buy-back deals — whether they are set for three, four or five years after the vehicle is supplied — help control the company's costs. It knows exactly how much that vehicle will cost per month, leaving drivers and fuel as the two most variable costs.

'Admin costs are very small, minute actually,' says Edward Stobart. 'Maintenance costs are very important to us; we need monthly costs, so we operate a strict policy of either maintaining trucks in-house at our own workshops or having this done by the manufacturer at a guaranteed cost over an agreed period of time.' Those guaranteed maintenance contracts come from Stobart's buying power. The more trucks it buys from one manufacturer, the better the price it is likely to secure.

There are major financial advantages in replacing the trucks after three years. They don't need to be repainted, they will only be halfway through their second set of tyres and they should only require servicing and MoT tests. At that age, something would be very wrong if they required replacement engines or gearboxes, but after three years parts like compressors may start to fail. 'The cost-effective time to replace is after three years,' says Edward Stobart, 'provided you do the miles. We average around 110,000 miles per vehicle per year. If it runs fewer miles, then we would keep it longer. The tyre-replacement theory goes out if we're not doing that many miles.'

Some vehicles will clock up far higher

Above: Leyland DAF 95 M100 (M100 ESL) *Sarah Elizabeth* alongside Iveco EuroStar H004 (M4 ESL) *Twiggy* and Scania R113M M113 SAO. **Mike Greenwood**

Below: Seddon Atkinson Strato H454 (K454 DAO) *Pippa.* **Garry Donnelly**

mileages, but the fleet is swapped around to achieve something closer to the average. Thus a vehicle may start out working on the most intensive trunking work (doing something like 800 miles a day — equivalent to 300,000 miles a year) for six months, and then move on to much less intensive work after that.

If the company's buying power was taken to its logical conclusion, Stobart's would operate only one type of truck across its whole fleet. But other considerations stop that from being done. 'It wouldn't be right because we need to have competition between manufacturers. One type of truck might not be good for us one year, but the manufacturer might then change something to make it better.' So it's important to shop around and even try trucks or batches of trucks to compare its most common types and makes with potential alternatives.

Eddie Stobart's managers look beyond the merits and costs of the vehicle and pay particular attention to the apparent strength of the manufacturer itself. 'Can it supply what we want, when we want it? Will it be around to support it? It's important to us that the people making our trucks and trailers, and the banks too, are strong. We recognise that they need to make a margin on the product they provide if they're going to survive,' says Edward Stobart.

'That's where UK truck manufacturers lost out with the bigger UK truck fleets. There was a fear that if they were not around, the warranty support on the truck would go with them. And that's where the major European manufacturers have stolen a march in this country.' The Stobart fleet is almost entirely made up of trucks from the major European manufacturers — many of whom also are the world's biggest truck makers — and these are makes which established themselves in Britain while Edward Stobart and others found the home manufacturers unable to take their new rivals seriously enough to fight back on equal terms.

The current fleet — and the rate of replacement means that this is a steadily changing picture — is approximately 40% Volvo with substantial numbers of MANs and Scanias and rather fewer Mercedes-Benz, Iveco, DAF and Renault trucks. The Volvo content reflects the manufacturer's dominance of the market for the size of tractor units and drawbar vehicles that make up most of the Stobart fleet; as it says, that doesn't mean that Volvo trucks are necessarily the best on the market, but equally it shows they are far from the worst. Had Volvo proceeded with plans to acquire Scania in 1999/2000, Stobart's would likely have only bought one of the two marques in the longer term, as it likes to maintain separate, independent sources of supply.

Company policy is to concentrate the types into certain depots, rather than having them mixed across the country. Sometimes this will be because of the proximity of a manufacturer's service dealer to a particular depot, as it helps to reduce the dead mileage clocked up when diverting for a minor repair like replacing a damaged mirror. It also makes it far easier to swap drivers between trucks — a key part of the Stobart approach to the efficient use of the fleet on trunk runs between depots — if they are switching between near-identical vehicles. And if there is only one type of truck at a depot, there is less chance of drivers trying to insist on being put in a different type from that first allocated to them.

Consequently, Volvos are allocated to Carlisle and Warrington, the Yorkshire depots at Wakefield and Sherburn-in-Elmet, the Midlands depots at Crick and Burton and the South East sites at Watford, Harlow and Beckton; the MANs are in three main clusters, at Penrith, Workington, Carlisle and Glasgow, at Bristol and at Stamford, Lincolnshire. The main Scania bases are at Poole, Bridgwater, Sittingbourne, Wakefield

Above: A Leyland DAF 95 drawbar unit, M575 (M575 RAO) *Dawn Louise.*
Mike Greenwood

and Leicester, while all 40 Mercedes-Benz were allocated to Warrington. Carlisle is the only base with Renaults, and the diminishing DAF fleet is mostly at Carlisle and Warrington. One of the most unusual vehicles in the fleet is a solitary, eye-catching bonneted Scania T114 at Carlisle, vehicle H777 *Kerry Jane*, delivered in 1998.

Among the most typically distinctive Stobart vehicles are its 18m drawbar combinations — rigid trucks with trailers, and a type used more by Stobart than by most other UK fleets. Today, there are fewer than 80 and current thinking is that these will gradually be phased out. Their big benefit in carrying high-volume loads came when articulated semi-trailers were limited to 12m, but that advantage has been reduced by the new 13.5m limit which provides more load space without the extra tyre and fuel-consumption costs associated with drawbar outfits.

Around 90% of Stobart's trailers have Boalloy bodywork, most of them built on Crane Fruehauf chassis, although there also are some with Montracon and M&G chassis. It aims to replace these after seven years (10 years used to be the average) and is

interested in reducing this closer to five years. Some curtain-sided trailers have step-frame chassis to maximise load space.

Although most trailers are curtain-siders (as mentioned in the separate chapter on the subject, there are temperature-controlled trailers in the Eddie Stobart International fleet), there are other types. Low-loaders are used for plant-hire movements, including work in the railway sector; the company's first double-deck dry goods van trailer was introduced in 1996 for movements in and out of mainland Europe, and around the same time the first 12 of a new design of Montracon bulk-tipping trailers were introduced to take scrap metal to recycling sites and return with steel plate or coil.

More recently, the company has developed a side-opening box trailer with concertina-type folding doors along the full length of the sides. The first of its kind in the UK, this fully-insulated vehicle can be opened or closed by one driver in less than a minute and is designed for ambient or chilled food distribution. It could mark a move away from curtain-siders for at least part of the Stobart operation.

Below: Leyland DAF drawbar outfit M164 (J754 ARM). *Garry Donnelly*

Above: Carlisle-based Leyland DAF 85.400 *Susan Anne.* **Garry Donnelly**

Below: Leyland DAF 85.330 H006 (L920 KRM) covered in Cumbrian snow.
Garry Donnelly

Below: M568 (M568 RAO) *Linsey Marie*, a Leyland DAF drawbar vehicle with DAF's Space Cab sleeper cab layout where the driver climbs up to the sleeping bunk at night. The layout maximises the space available for load carrying. *Garry Donnelly*

Below: H019 (J736 XHH) *Seonad* was a Leyland DAF 95 tractor unit with the sleeping compartment behind the driver's seat. Alongside is *Helga*, an appropriately German-named MAN G90 light delivery truck. The G90 used the same cab as Volkswagen's smaller LT van and began life in 1976 as the jointly-marketed MAN-VW MT. *Garry Donnelly*

Above: H006 (L920 KRM) *Alexa Sarah*, a 330hp Leyland DAF 85 tractor unit and curtain-sided trailer. During 1999, Paccar ceased using the Leyland name (which was retained largely for the British market) and the products are now branded simply as DAFs. *Garry Donnelly*

Below: M636 (M636 TAO) *Maureen Pamela* leads a line-up of Leyland DAF 95s. *Mike Greenwood*

Above: H012 (N12 ESL) *Taome*, a Leyland DAF 85 tractor and curtain-sided tri-axle trailer. **Garry Donnelly**

Below: A winter scene with drawbar outfit M316 (H175 TAO) *Fiona Helen*, a 330hp Leyland DAF 95. **Garry Donnelly**

Above: M576 (M576 RAO) *Elaine Patricia*, a Leyland DAF 95 drawbar combination.
Garry Donnelly

Below: Six-wheel drawbar rigid M202 (L2 DGM) *Jo Beth*, a Leyland DAF 95 360hp.
Mike Greenwood

Above: H428 (K428 DAO) *Wendy May*, a Seddon Atkinson Strato 17.33TC in winter sunshine. *Garry Donnelly*

THE MAIN TRUCK TYPES OPERATED BY EDDIE STOBART
DAF 85 and 95

DAF, based at Eindhoven in the Netherlands, was a trailer manufacturer before it started making trucks in 1950. In 1986, it acquired control of British manufacturer Leyland's truck business in a joint venture known as Leyland DAF. After the failure of the original DAF company in 1993, the two companies again went into separate ownership, but retained a close working relationship. DAF, rescued by a consortium of Dutch interests, was acquired in 1996 by Seattle-based Paccar, the largest American-owned truck manufacturer, which went on later to acquire Leyland and which had owned Foden of the UK since 1980.

The DAF 85, launched in 1993/4, is powered by the manufacturer's own 11.6-litre engine, a design developed from one of Leyland's engines and manufactured under a licensing agreement first signed in 1955 — long before DAF had any financial stake in

Leyland. Stobart's 85s are tractor units.

The DAF 95 was launched in 1987 and uses a cab developed jointly by DAF and the Spanish ENASA group, which sold its truck manufacturing business to Iveco in 1990. This so-called Cabtec driving cab was also fitted on the Seddon Atkinson Strato tractor unit which used to figure in the Stobart fleet, as Seddon Atkinson was part of the ENASA empire. In its original form, it uses the same 11.6-litre engine as the DAF 85, but the 12.6-litre-engined 95XF was introduced in 1997. Stobart has operated DAF 95 drawbar outfits and 95XF tractor units.

Iveco

Iveco is an acronym for Industrial Vehicles Corporation, and is the truck and bus division of Italy's FIAT. It is one of Europe's largest truck manufacturers, building vehicles in Italy, Germany, Spain and England, and engines in France. The EuroTech was first launched in 1992 — in Britain the following year — and is available in versions ranging

Continued on page 38

Above: Eddie Stobart Ltd may be a child of the 1970s, but that hasn't stopped it indulging in some harmless nostalgia for an earlier age. *Lesley Christine*, this six-wheel Atkinson with a 1948 Stirlingshire registration mark, is in a period rendition of the red, green and gold colours introduced gradually during the 1970s. Behind it are two inflatable bouncy castles in the shape of modern Eddie Stobart lorries. **Mike Greenwood**

Below: Caldbeck, southwest of Carlisle and northwest of Penrith, was the haulage business's home for seven years before it moved into Carlisle. Its former base is commemorated on the preserved Atkinson. **Mike Greenwood**

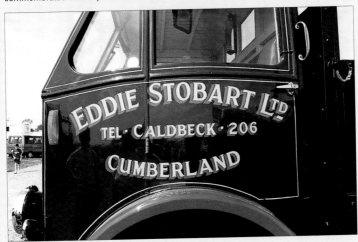

Above: Iveco EuroTechs M594/89 (M594/89 RHH) *Lizzy* and *Tania Maureen* side by side. **Garry Donnelly**

Below: A wintry view of Seddon Atkinson tractor unit H302 (H259 SHH) *Carol Brenda*. **Garry Donnelly**

Above: Carlisle-based MAN F2000 H1648 (T648 JHH) *Emma Nicole* is typical of the tractor unit/curtain-sided semi-trailer combination bought by Stobart in recent years. ***Alan Millar***

Below: Still awaiting the allocation of a girl's name, then-new MAN F2000 H1610 (T610 JHH) helped publicise Stobart's at an event. The F2000 was introduced in 1994 and uses the same design of cab as the F90 which was first launched seven years earlier. ***Garry Donnelly***

Above: Curtain-sided trailers, with their built-in load restraints and speedy loading characteristics, helped Eddie Stobart revolutionise the service it offered to British industry. In this 1994 view, Volvo FL10 H512 (L512 MHH) *Karla* is loaded by fork-lift truck at the end of an exhibition. **Mike Greenwood**

Below: Some of Stobart's truck names are appropriate to the types of vehicle. This French-built Renault Major R340h has a French girl's name. H146 (L146 NHH) *Angelique* is seen attached to a low-loader trailer used to carry plant and sometimes other trucks. **Mike Greenwood**

Above and Below: Although they are totally separate businesses, James Irlam of Cheshire and Eddie Stobart share one major contract and also have similar operating standards and livery styles. Irlam's mixed fleet includes Leyland DAF 85 tractors and curtain-sided tri-axle trailers. ***Leyland DAF***

from 18-tonne local-delivery trucks up to 44-tonne intercontinental tractors. It is powered by a 7.7-litre Iveco engine. Stobart has evaluated tractor units and 32-tonne drawbar vehicles. In 1990, Iveco acquired ENASA of Spain and its UK subsidiary Seddon Atkinson, a Stobart supplier until recent years.

MAN

MAN — the initials are for Maschinenfabrik Augsburg Nürnberg — is the smaller of Germany's two major truck and bus manufacturers. In 1990, it acquired Austrian truck maker Steyr and went on to buy British manufacturer ERF — a significant Stobart supplier in the recent past — and Poland's Star in 2000.

Below: You get some idea of the imposing scale of a modern truck from this ground-level view of MAN F2000 H1671 (W671 PAO) *Candy.* **Alan Millar**

Above: H528 (L528 MHH) *Anneke Jayne*, an ERF EC10, was photographed in 1994. Cheshire-based ERF was the last British-owned volume builder of heavy trucks and was still in family ownership when the EC was introduced in 1993. The manufacturer was taken over by Canada's Western Star group in 1996 and then became part of MAN in 2000. **Mike Greenwood**

Three Scania R124L 360hp tractor units, with H321 (P321 DHH) *Maimie* nearest the camera. Scania's position as a Stobart supplier could have been threatened had Volvo succeeded in its attempt to acquire its Swedish rival. ***Scania (GB)***

Above: A Leyland DAF 95, a Renault Major and an ERF EC10. ***Mike Greenwood***

Below: Iveco EuroTech H587 (M587 RHH) *Shani* attached to a low-loader trailer carrying two Volvo FL10 tractor units. Substantial fuel savings can be made by moving trucks this way between depots rather than under their own power. ***Garry Donnelly***

Left: Carlisle-based MAN F2000 H1648 (T648 JHH) *Emma Nicole* viewed head-on.
Alan Millar

Most MANs in the Stobart fleet are F2000 tractor units from a range introduced in 1993, but the small fleet of rigid local-delivery vehicles includes M2000 models with Steyr-designed cabs. In 2000, MAN launched its new-generation TG-A (for Trucknology Generation) tractor unit range with a completely new cab and heavy reliance on electronics for engine management and braking.

Mercedes-Benz

Germany's — and the world's — largest heavy-truck manufacturer is a relatively small-scale supplier to Stobart's. It only secured its first significant order in 1996, for 20 tractor units to its now discontinued SK design. It has since supplied small batches of the newer Actros tractor unit, introduced from 1996, and these operate from the Warrington base which also was home to the SKs. Several are in United Glass livery. The van fleet includes Mercedes-Benz Sprinters.

Above: One of the small fleet of Mercedes-Benz Actros 1840 tractor units is H251 (P251 CRM) *Mary Anne*. Others are in United Glass green livery. *Garry Donnelly*

43

Above: Looking more like an American truck than a European one is H777 (S777 ESL) *Kerry Jane,* the solitary bonneted Scania T114L with 380hp engine. Its layout offers no great advantages over the company's standard R-cabbed Scanias, but it helps draw attention to the Stobart business. *Scania (GB)*

Below Left: A 1994 view of the historic Atkinson on a low-loader trailer behind Renault Major tractor H146 (L146 NHH) *Angelique*. **Mike Greenwood**

Below: The earlier style of curtain-sider livery, with script-style Eddie Stobart Ltd names and a clear statement that the company is based in Carlisle, Cumbria. The tractor unit is Volvo FL10 H626 (M626 TAO) *Audrey* and the year is 1996. **Mike Greenwood**

Renault

Renault Véhicules Industriels, the French automotive giant's truck division, was acquired by Volvo in 2000. Before that happened, Stobart's took small batches of two types of Renault trucks into its fleet for evaluation. It took three Magnum top-weight tractor units to a futuristic design introduced in 1990 with a highly-distinctive tall, flat-floored cab. It also acquired nine Premium tractor units.

Top: A French name and a catchy Select registration help distinguish H015 Renault Magnum tractor unit *Gigi*. It is powered by a 12-litre 390hp Renault engine, and, as can be seen from this photograph, a distinguishing feature of the Magnum is its forward-mounted axle and steps up behind rather than in front of the wheel. *Garry Donnelly*

Above: Rear view of a Renault Magnum-hauled semi-trailer. *Mike Greenwood*

Above: Side view of H101, one of the Renault Magnum tractor units acquired for evaluation. **Mike Greenwood**

Below: A more conventional Renault design is the Premium, of which H277 (P277 DHH) *Susan Shirley* is an example. **Garry Donnelly**

Scania

After over 100 years as an independent company, Scania — the smaller of Sweden's two international truck manufacturers — is in the process of being acquired by Volkswagen. Stobart is a long-standing Scania customer and has been replacing its older-generation 3-series Scanias with the 4-series introduced in 1995. Most are R114L and R124L tractor units with conventional — by British standards — cab-over-engine layout. But there is also one T114L bonneted model with the same cab fitted behind the engine; this eye-catching truck was bought in 1997 for evaluation and met a particular operational need to use a 41ft rather than 45ft trailer. There also are some rigid Scania delivery trucks.

Above: Scania R113M tractor unit M113 SAO *Tracey Mary* in 1995. ***Mike Greenwood***

Right: The typical rear view of a Stobart truck, designed to convey a clear message to the decision-making drivers of following cars. ***Alan Millar***

Below: Scania's large badges mean that truck names are sometimes squeezed into a smaller space than on other types. H322 (P322 DHH) *Nicola* is a 400hp R124L with a step-frame curtain-sided trailer. Step-frame trailers, built to Stobart's design by Don-Bur, were introduced in 1994 for high volume loads. They are fitted with a swinging deck floor which enables goods to be stacked two pallets high. Their low centre of gravity also enhances stability. *Garry Donnelly*

Above: A line-up of Scania R114L tractor units, with H1715 (V715 DRM) *Trisanne* nearest the camera. *Garry Donnelly*

Volvo

The main truck make in the Stobart fleet currently is Volvo, now one of the world's largest truck manufacturers, with major plants in Sweden, Belgium, North and South America.

Older examples are 9.6-litre-engined FL10s, a design first introduced in 1985. These are being replaced by new-generation 12.1-litre-engined FH12 tractor units of a design launched in 1993 and the similar, but lower-cabbed 9.6-litre-engined FM10 introduced in 1998 may also join the Fleet.

Above: Carlisle-based Volvo FH12 drawbar unit M1405 (R405 WRM) *Carolyn Louise* viewed head-on. ***Alan Millar***

Left: The historic Atkinson named *Lesley Christine.* **Mike Greenwood**

Below: When it's economically justified, accident-damaged trucks are repaired and returned to service. Volvo FL10 tractor L484 LHH *Britt* awaited a decision on its future when this photograph was taken. **Garry Donnelly**

Right: Volvo FL10 tractor unit H818 (N818 VAO) *Ingrid* and a curtain-sided tri-axle trailer. **Garry Donnelly**

Below: Carlisle-based Volvo FH12 drawbar unit M1405 (R405 WRM) *Carolyn Louise* typifies the vehicles which used to form the backbone of the fleet. **Alan Millar**

A selection of some of the Corgi models of Eddie Stobart vehicles available to collectors. **Corgi**

Above: Volvo FH12 tractor unit H009 (P9 ESL) *Portia Louise* with a tri-axle van-bodied trailer. **Garry Donnelly**

Below: Volvo FL10 tractor G971 ORM *Catrina.* **Garry Donnelly**

Above: Volvo FH12 H1351 (S251 RAO) *Kaitlyn*. **Garry Donnelly**

Below: H884 (N884 VAO) *Moira* is a Burnley-based Volvo FL10. **Garry Donnelly**

Above: A Tango-liveried ERF with orange lining around the chassis sides to show that this is a Stobart truck. *Mike Greenwood*

Right: Knauf-liveried Scania P114CB F748 (P748 FAO) *Barbara Ann* was the first eight-wheeler for the Stobart fleet. It carries an Atlas truck-mounted crane at the back to unload plasterboard at building sites. *Scania (GB)*

Above: Volvo FL10 M545 PAO *Patricia Anne.* **Garry Donnelly**

Below: Volvo FH12 H1379 (T379 KHH) *Maddison.* **Garry Donnelly**

Above: Carrying the same name as former US President Bill Clinton's daughter is Volvo FH12 H500 (N500 ESL) *Chelsea*. **Garry Donnelly**

Below: Volvo FL10 H876 (N876 VAO) *Conchita* with a curtain-sided trailer in the older style of signwriting. **Garry Donnelly**

Above: Efficient operation of the fleet is reinforced by the strategic positioning of the depot network. Some sites have warehousing, some are transport-only sites and many accommodate both sides of the business. *Mike Greenwood*

Below: The Carlisle head office in 1995. Although kept in immaculate condition, with Stobart-liveried carpeting, it remains a modest home to a highly successful business very much in the public eye. *Mike Greenwood*

Above: Volvo FL10 H869 (N869 VAO) *Yvette.* **Garry Donnelly**

Below: Two Volvo FL10 tractors, H557 (M557 PAO) *Blanca* and H545 (M545 PAO) *Patricia Anne.* **Garry Donnelly**

Below: One of the newer drawbar outfits in the fleet is attached to six-wheel Volvo FH12 M1408 (R408 WRM) *Gail Frances.* **Garry Donnelly**

Bottom: Volvo FL10 tractor unit H491 (L491 LHH) *Mariette.* **Mike Greenwood**

3. FROM BRUNSWICK GREEN TO STOBART GREEN - EVOLUTION OF THE LIVERY

Above: Simple identity of the Stobart 'S' chevron and crossed flags of Europe and Irish-style tricolour. ***Alan Millar***

The now-familiar Eddie Stobart livery didn't happen overnight, nor was it the product of an expensive design consultancy. It evolved over the company's early years as a modest-sized haulier and owes a lot to Edward Stobart's own sense of how his lorries should look.

Like many self-made hauliers, Stobart remembers extraordinary details about his first vehicles and can tell you that his first curtain-siders — the vehicles whose big canvas sides provided the medium to display the Eddie Stobart name in big bold type — were trailers No 4 and No 5. That was in 1976. Trailers No 1 and No 2 were bulk tippers and No 3 was a flatbed. Over the next

year, he added more flatbeds from British Steel and continued running bulk tippers for a major customer, but the curtain-siders literally had the canvas he needed to carry moving advertisements for the business.

The first curtain-siders had gold script-type signwriting, but this subsequently changed to the block capitals used today. For some time, the fleet also carried the words 'Express Haulage', 'Carlisle' and phone numbers, but it now calls itself an Express Road Haulage Specialist and Carlisle no longer appears on the back as the company came to believe that such a northerly base might deter potential customers in southern

Continued on page 72

Above: The simpler, more modern fleetname style, with Eddie Stobart Ltd is bold italics and without any reference to Carlisle or Cumbria. The truck is a Leyland DAF 95 drawbar and the year is 1994. *Mike Greenwood*

Below: New trucks for the Eddie Stobart fleet are delivered from their factories in white with black chassis components. The company then repaints them in its own workshops, and paints them back into white, but with red chassis componentry, when they are sold back to manufacturers' dealers. This is a Scania R113M tractor unit. *Mike Greenwood*

Right: The truck-naming policy began in 1974 with a DAF christened *Twiggy*. This is a later holder of the same name, Iveco EuroStar H004 (M4 ESL). The EuroStar is Iveco's top-of-the-range truck, with a wider cab than the EuroTech. *Garry Donnelly*

Above: Side view of MAN F2000 H1671 (W671 PAO) *Candy,* showing the 'S' logo and flags. ***Alan Millar***

Below: Rear-view of a trailer. Some of the latest in the fleet carry the www.eddiestobart.co.uk website address. *Mike Greenwood*

Above: The many girls commemorated on Stobart trucks include *Mae Janet* on a Volvo FH12... *Alan Millar*

England, where more and more of its business is generated today.

At the start, the livery was all-over mid-Brunswick green, but it changed soon after to deep Brunswick green, probably because that happened to be the choice of a vehicle supplier at the time. As it began to exercise more control over its image, the company added Post Office red. It was in 1974 that the effect was completed with the addition of white. Edward Stobart had bought a DAF 2800 and resolved to paint it differently, so had a white band added to the cab. 'I looked at it once and felt it was just too dull, so we introduced a white band and a white roof.'

Today, ICI supplies those specially-mixed colours by the names of Stobart Green, Stobart Red and Stobart Gold. Trucks are supplied in factory-finished white and repainted into fleet colours at the company's own paintshop in Carlisle using up-to-date spraying and baking technology; the paintshop also keeps existing vehicles up to

the required standard of presentation. Before a truck is returned to its supplier at the end of its life in the Stobart fleet, it is painted back into white with a red bumper and chassis so there is no danger of another owner passing it off as a Stobart vehicle.

AND THE FIRST WAS CHRISTENED *TWIGGY*

The DAF 2800 also introduced another of the most distinctive features of the Stobart identity. It was named *Twiggy* after the model-turned-singer who had a song in the charts at the time. She may not be aware of it, but Twiggy set the trend for naming the whole fleet after women. Edward Stobart is refreshingly honest about why the first one bore her name. 'She looked nice on television. She looked a nice, beautiful lady and Twiggy is a nice sharp name. Not one of the usual ones.'

Twiggy was followed by trucks named after three other of the owner's favourite

Above: . . . *Hyacinth* on an MAN F2000 . . . **Mike Greenwood**

Above: . . . *Pamela Elizabeth* on another FH12 . . . **Mike Greenwood**

female singers of the time: *Dolly* (for Dolly Parton), *Suzi* (for Suzi Quatro) and *Tammy* (for the late Tammy Wynette). Others have included *Tina* (for Tina Turner) and *Bonnie* (for Bonnie Tyler). After that, he broadened the choice by inviting drivers to choose names for the growing fleet — usually those of their wives, girlfriends or daughters — but this began to cause operational problems. 'It became a nightmare when drivers were swapped from one vehicle to another and a lot of them wanted to take the name with them, so we stopped that.' There also were those awkward moments when drivers

Right: . . . *Marion* on an Iveco EuroTech . . . *Garry Donnelly*

Below . . . *Henrietta* on a Seddon Atkinson Strato. . . *Garry Donnelly*

Above: . . . an Iveco EuroTech named *Gwyneth* . . .**Mike Greenwood**

changed girlfriends or wives and wanted to change the name of their truck. The boss was back naming trucks after people he admired until he began — understandably — to run out of inspiration.

He passed the job on to his secretary, Deborah Rodgers, who has since turned this into one of the many continuing responsibilities in her role looking after the marketing and promotion of the business. She is custodian of the waiting list of between 200 and 300 names due to be allocated to trucks in the fleet. Thanks to the Eddie Stobart Fan Club and members of the general public, names come in weekly to be added to the list. Provided suitable names haven't already been used on a current truck, they will be added to the list and used in

Right: . . . and a Volvo FL10 named *Cressida*. **Mike Greenwood**

Below: Washing equipment has been installed at the depots to help keep the fleet as clean as possible. In this June 1995 view, Leyland DAF 95 tractor unit J758 XHH *Diorbhail* is spruced up ready for its next journey. **Mike Greenwood**

rotation. Urgent requests are always considered and may be allowed to jump the queue. Similarly, famous topical names will be used ahead of more routine names when circumstances dictate.

Along with the livery and the girls' names is a fastidious attention to the detailed upkeep of the company's image. Just as drivers must wear uniforms to the required standard, offices and depots are maintained to impeccable standards of presentation, and the trucks are washed regularly. Edward Stobart believes that it was the cleanliness as much as the livery itself which first attracted people's attention to his vehicles.

'At first our vehicles were noticed because people were used to seeing dirty trucks.' he once told *Looking Good* magazine. 'I think it seems more professional to run clean trucks and the nice thing is that other companies have followed suit. I've always been fussy about things and I've always had very clean vehicles right from the start.

'I used to wash all the trucks myself and I still don't let the drivers wash them. We want professional drivers. We don't expect them to come back and wash their vehicles.'

Below: Scania 114L H134 (W134 ORM) was still awaiting a name when this photograph was taken in 2000. *Garry Donnelly*

4. EUROPE - THE NEW OPPORTUNITY FOR GROWTH

Eddie Stobart's move into international haulage was begun in an uncharacteristic way for a company which has grown organically since its formation in 1970. It bought another business.

The company which trades today from Warrington as Eddie Stobart International was previously called Jenerite, and was based in Stoke-on-Trent when it was acquired early in 1998. As well as changing the name and base, Stobart's also replaced Jenerite's maroon livery with its own green, white and red; within 18 months, it had grown. Turnover was up from £4 million to £20 million, and the fleet was increased from 20 to 50 vehicles; another 100 trucks were

Below: Yet-to-be-named, Belgian-based Volvo FH12 H1176 (SRR 421), complete with 'Eddie Stobart NV' lettering above the passenger's door on this left-hand-drive truck. *Garry Donnelly*

Above: The Belgian fleet is being given appropriate names. Scania R114L H1180 (SNA 320) is *Marie Jeanne*. **Garry Donnelly**

added in mid-2000. In addition, at least 100 vehicles and their owner-drivers are contracted regularly to carry its freight.

Eddie Stobart International operates in two markets, hauling curtain-siders and temperature-controlled trailers — the latter a market this small division of the company has broken into ahead of the parent company. Indeed, the first Gray & Adams temperature-controlled trailers were built primarily for a major contract secured with the NAAFI in 1999 to deliver over 1,500 movements of foodstuffs a year to 63

military bases in Germany. These trailers have a unique system of longitudinal and transverse bulkheads which allow the transport of a mix of frozen, chilled and ambient products; the configuration can be adjusted and the size and temperature of each compartment altered to suit a range of roll-cage consignments.

The first Eddie Stobart International depot in Europe was opened near Ghent in Belgium, a location selected because of its proximity to what in effect is a major crossroads in the Continental European highway network, and the Belgian network has grown to three depots.

The International business has taken the Eddie Stobart name across much of Europe, with deliveries to such far-flung destinations as Greece, Macedonia, Kosovo, Italy, Hungary, Poland, Germany, the Netherlands, Sweden, Austria, Spain and France. The expectation is that, as this business grows, a network of European depots will be opened to provide a similar level of coverage to that which has made the company so successful in Britain.

The Belgian fleet is registered there rather than in the UK and is managed by a combination of British managers and Belgian administrative staff. The longer-term aim is to teach Belgian — and other — nationals to work with the British management to develop what is a completely separate arm of the business. Other European expansion could see the company establish joint ventures in Poland and Hungary.

Having built up the British core fleet, Stobart now sees Europe as the area for its fastest future growth. This is partly because of the highly-publicised difference between British and some mainland European tax levels, both on trucks and on diesel fuel. From the company's point of view, it makes sense to concentrate the next phase of expansion in mainland European markets where these tax rates are lower, rather than run international operations entirely from Britain. On the other hand, this isn't quite the same as the 'flagging-out' policy adopted by some other British operators which have re-registered substantial parts of their fleets in countries like Belgium, the Netherlands or Luxembourg to take advantage of lower taxes. The UK-based fleet continues to be registered in its homeland.

The move into Europe isn't likely to result in any significant difference in the types of vehicles operated by Eddie Stobart. After all, it standardises on Swedish and German manufacturers' products and the final choice of trucks for Eddie Stobart International is expected to be determined by which of those manufacturers has the most convenient local depots.

Above: Set against a background of snow-dusted Border hills, Carlisle-based Volvo FH12 drawbar unit M1405 (R405 WRM) *Carolyn Louise* pauses at Abington services on the M74 in South Lanarkshire. **Alan Millar**

5. THE EDDIE STOBART FAN CLUB

Above: Eddie Stobart trucks are popular with model makers and collectors.
Mike Greenwood

Where most large businesses have substantial marketing and public-relations departments with budgets to match, Eddie Stobart has its 20,000-strong fan club. It's a priceless asset which, like so much else of this company, was born almost by accident.

In 1989, the musician Jools Holland gave an interview to someone in which he said his one recreation on tour was spotting Eddie Stobart trucks. It was picked up by BBC disc jockeys on Radio 1 and Radio 2 who asked listeners to ring in with their latest sighting of an 'Eddie' truck. DJ Bruno Brooks once said: 'Every time I mention Eddie Stobart on the air, the phones in the studio light up.' The national sport of 'Eddie spotting' was begun with people being encouraged to while away

their hours on the national motorway network by seeing how many Eddie Stobart trucks they 'copped' on their journey.

Letters started to trickle into the head office in Carlisle. The trickle grew into a stream. The stream grew into a flood. It got to a point when the company began to appreciate what a positive monster had been created. 'We were getting that many letters in the post we thought we'd better get involved in this,' Edward Stobart told a newspaper interviewer in 1999.

'People have enrolled babies. We have children around two years of age up to a lady of 97. We have fans in Europe and even in New Zealand. Why? I don't know.

'The fan club was meant to be free, but it

Above: An Eddie Stobart Promotions Iveco EuroCargo mobile sales and exhibition unit.
Mike Greenwood

has been such a cost to the company that we've had to impose a charge of £6 a year (£8 for the first year) and that only covers materials. It doesn't cover our labour. We have two or three people who do nothing except the fan club,' he told that same interviewer. 'But we've got a lot from it and it's good for the transport industry. We've heard some lovely stories. We've taken people to weddings and we've had requests to take them to funerals.' It's also been known to arrange birthday treats — and here we can be talking people well into middle age — where a club member is taken for a ride in a Stobart truck. Conducted tours are provided around company facilities to provide behind-the-scenes insights into how the Stobart business operates.

'Fan club members write in and suggest ideas, especially new ideas for merchandise, and we're delighted when people write in with nice comments about our drivers and what they like about our trucks,' adds

Edward Stobart. Affection for all things Stobart is such that, when one of the company's trucks appeared on national television hanging precariously from a flyover parapet after it was caught in winter gales, shoals of 'get well' cards flowed into Carlisle from club members anxious for the condition of the truck. The driver, happily, had escaped unhurt.

For the membership fee, the fan club provides an up-to-date official fleet manual, listing the trucks in the current fleet, along with a membership card, a badge, a car sticker, a calendar each year and a copy of the quarterly *Fan Club News*. The newsletter keeps the far-flung club membership in touch and is very much a product of the people so fascinated by this truck fleet. There are poems by members, letters from members, drawings, computer-generated illustrations and pictures of truck models by members (especially by children) and there are stories about club members.

These stories include how Julie Wilkinson from Bristol achieved her ambition of visiting the company's headquarters in Carlisle, basing herself and husband in the nearby Kingstown Hotel where, if it rained, they could indulge in 'Eddie spotting' from their hotel room window. Another tells of the New Zealand football fans who wear sponsored Carlisle United jerseys in deckchair-like vertical stripes of corporate green, white, red and gold with 'Eddie Stobart' names.

Fan club members also gain privileged access to the company's website — www.eddiestobart.co.uk.

The fan club phenomenon has given birth to an ever-increasing range of merchandise that celebrates the company and is available through a subsidiary company, Eddie Stobart Promotions, which helps the company control the use of its memorable image. These include a growing range of Corgi 1:50, 1:64 and 1:36 scale diecast models of trucks, trailers, vans and cars in the familiar livery; modellers' licence has expanded this range to include types like the Atkinson Borderer, Foden S21, Bedford S and TK, Thames Trader and Leyland Octopus, which may not have run in real life in Stobart colours but show how they might have appeared had the company been formed a few decades before 1970. Recent releases include a three-wheel Reliant Regal van in 1:36 scale to represent a vehicle owned by one of the fan club members, while there are also vehicles in the various customers' contract liveries.

There are limited-edition signed prints of paintings showing trucks in eye-catching locations and a whole range of clothing and mementos; clothing includes sweatshirts, rally jackets, fleeces, tee-shirts and umbrellas, while mementos include various branded teddy bears, greetings cards, cigarette lighters, pens, cassettes, videos,

mugs, balloons, a Wade Ceramics money box in the shape of an MAN truck, and even tea bags.

Tea bags? The company took the view that tea has been so long associated with lorry drivers that there was money to be made by developing its own brand in green, gold and red Stobart Tea packs.

In a particularly astute move which may succeed in hooking some of the country's youngest citizens into the Stobart image, a 'Steady Eddie'-branded range of toys and associated goods has been developed, partly in conjunction with Corgi. This projects an image more like that of Thomas the Tank Engine, with named anthropomorphic vans and trucks (like Rick Van Rental, Jock the Tartan Tanker and a corporate-liveried Steady Eddie himself, who is also available as a ride-on toy). The range extends into educational toys, story books, puzzles, colouring books, children's mugs, tee-shirts and baseball caps.

The Steady Eddie character began in the story books, first written by Commercial Director Barrie Thomas and illustrated by Cumbrian artist Tim Ellis, and containing a strong road-safety message which helped win the endorsement of the Royal Society for the Prevention of Accidents. Marketing tie-ups have been secured through supermarkets and high-street retailers and also through the Little Chef roadside restaurant chain which, ironically, bans trucks from its parking areas.

Such has been the growth of the merchandising operation that, in June 1997, a dedicated Fan Club shop was opened in Carlisle's Castle Street, helping ease what was becoming a welcome problem of visitors beating a path to the out-of-town Carlisle headquarters site. There has been talk of opening other outlets around the country.

6. THE TRUCKS IN CUSTOMERS' COLOURS

While most Eddie Stobart vehicles are painted in the company's high-profile livery with its unmistakable fleetname spelt out across the sides of the trailers, there is more to the fleet than just those trucks. Some operate in customers' colours.

One of the road haulage industry's big achievements over the past 25 years and more has been to sell its services to industrial customers which previously ran their own fleets. As industrial competition

has intensified, many of these so-called 'own account' operators have been persuaded that their funds and expertise are better invested in their core businesses, leaving specialist logistics companies to provide transport, warehousing and distribution services tailored to their requirements.

Two — possibly three — features help identify Eddie Stobart vehicles in customers' colours. One is that they have the distinctive diagonal safety lines around the front and

Above: Volvo FH12 tractor unit H002 (V2 MGN) *Tina Ann* in red Mirror Group livery with diagonal bumper stripes, white stars on the panel above the headlights and white lined-out chassis sides to help show that this is a Stobart truck. It also has Eddie Stobart Ltd names above the fleetnumber on the cab door. The Select registration stands for Mirror Group Newspapers. *Garry Donnelly*

Above: A Pepsi-liveried ERF EC10 in an earlier style making no concession to the Stobart identity. *Mike Greenwood*

back bumpers, albeit in the customers' colours rather than standard red and white — along with a white star on the cab corners and white lining of the chassis sides. Another is that they carry the H-, M-, F- and V-prefixed fleetnumbers (for tractor unit, drawbar, rigid and van respectively) that appear on the main fleet. The third feature on some is a girl's name, not always as prominent as on the main fleet and sometimes picked by people within the customer's organisation.

The dedicated fleets include blue Scania rigids and artics operated by German-owned plasterboard manufacturer Knauf from the site at Sittingbourne where Knauf has its factory. Most of these are fitted with their own Moffett Mounty fork-lift trucks which can unload the lorries at building sites.

Volvo and Mercedes-Benz Actros articulated trucks operate in United Glass's green livery from both Warrington and Harlow, reflecting the fact that this high-profile customer — which used to have its own haulage company in the former Robson of Carlisle business — relies on Stobart's for all its warehousing requirements and for the bulk of its transport throughout the UK.

Another major client is Mirror Group, which has white-liveried vans and 10 red-liveried Volvo and MAN artics operating under Crick's control on overnight deliveries from the newspaper company's southern printing centre in Watford. This contract, secured in 1998, took Stobart's into a new market sector.

Other contract fleets are run on behalf of Schmalbach Lubeca and Gerber Foods.

7. THE ALL-IMPORTANT DEPOTS

One of the cornerstones of the Eddie Stobart success story is the company's determination to maintain control of the business and to have all the information it needs at its fingertips.

Three regional control centres, in Carlisle, Daventry and Bristol, are open 24 hours a day, 365 days a year. They plan the next day's traffic across the country and also keep track of where today's traffic is destined and how it is progressing. A dedicated controller — many are former drivers who understand the realities of modern traffic conditions — is allocated to each customer's traffic and

works either in one of the control rooms or on a large customer's own premises. It is their responsibility to respond to changing circumstances, letting customers know if a vehicle is delayed and making changes to suit a customer's altered requirements if, for example, a production line goes down and a delivery needs to be moved to a different location. This is just one of the ways in which companies like Stobart's fit in with today's practice of just-in-time delivery and manufacturing. The benefit of using ex-drivers for these jobs is that they respect drivers' positions when making requests and

won't make impossible demands, but also the drivers know they cannot pull the wool over the controllers' eyes and pretend that their realistic requests are unreasonable.

This sort of control depends on high-quality information technology. Communication with customers is by fax, phone, e-mail and electronic data interchange. Each vehicle is in phone contact with Central Control and in-cab systems allow drivers to update status reports on the progress of a delivery and can directly download proof of delivery information to Central Control. It means that if a customer phones for up-to-date information on when it can expect a delivery, a well-informed Stobart employee will provide that information almost instantly.

An essential part of the régime also sees every driver go through a full debriefing session each time he enters a depot.

In addition to the depot network, there is also a growing network of warehouses to provide part of the added-value service that helps Eddie Stobart maintain a distinctive edge for its customers. In over 4 million sq ft

Below: The smart condition of the fleet is paralleled by an equally fastidious approach to landscaping and maintenance of the depot premises. *Mike Greenwood*

Above: Exterior view of the Cook Street depot in Glasgow's Tradeston district, an area where motorway construction is likely to change the landscape over the next 10 years. ***Alan Millar***

of warehouse accommodation, the company manages goods on behalf of its customers, with consignments ranging from bulk to mixed products.

While many of the warehouses have large areas dedicated to a single customer's needs, others are shared between users who could not justify a warehouse area of their own. They are equipped with some of the latest materials-handling equipment and stock-control monitoring technology, with the full range of mechanised lifting equipment to ensure the quick and safe handling of customers' goods. Increasingly, specialist shunting vehicles similar to those found on busy docksides are being used to move trailers around the busiest depots.

Stobart's staff are sometimes contracted to carry out minor manufacturing roles in the warehouses, like inserting 'widgets' in empty beer cans stored at the Carlisle site.

Although the warehouses often generate traffic for the transport fleet or else hold goods already carried by Stobart lorries, some customers only buy into the warehousing service; they either have their own transport or rely on suppliers' transport to move their goods.

The approach to warehousing helps explain Edward Stobart's view of the company's current reliance on trucks. 'As business people, we're not fans of trucks on the road,' he says. 'We would use a catapult or a helicopter if it was the most cost-effective way of moving goods. We just go for the most practical vehicle which suits our operation.'

The largest warehousing site is one of two

operated by the company on the Daventry International Rail Freight Terminal site at Crick, Northamptonshire. This 700,000sq ft site is close to the M1/M6/A14 motorway and trunk road intersection and was opened in two phases, the first in November 1997 by the Princess Royal. It is a prime site within the most sought-after corner of the country for businesses involved in transport and distribution. The warehousing is on the rail-connected DIRFT South complex, while there is an operational depot at DIRFT West.

Crick is also home to Stobart's pallet hub, where palletised loads from around the country are exchanged between lorries to maintain a next-day delivery service throughout Britain. The pallet-hub concept was begun in 1997 at the Burton-upon-Trent warehouse, and is modelled on the way that express-parcels companies provide their guaranteed-delivery services.

The second-largest warehouse is the 500,000sq ft former Leyland Bus factory at Lillyhall, near Workington in West Cumbria. The 50-acre site ceased building buses when Volvo shut the plant in 1993 and has been refurbished in partnership with development agencies and the Cumbria Marketing Initiative. It's something of a statement, for, although Stobart's depends on the parts of England and Wales south of the M62 trans-Pennine motorway for most of its business, it also is keen to show pride in its Cumbrian base by investing in the area. The object of the Lillyhall site is to provide a state-of-the-art distribution service for companies based in West Cumbria while also providing space for incoming companies to lease industrial space for their own requirements. As such, it hopes to be able to encourage manufacturing on to a site first developed in the early 1970s as part of a Government-sponsored regional development policy. Customers already attracted into Lillyhall include Historical Collections, Lawson Mardon Packaging, Ellay Enfield, Hoechst, Reiber, Wolf and J. Dixon.

The company's other major site — and its newest — is at Sherburn-in-Elmet, east of the junctions between the A1(M) and M1 and M62 motorways. Warehousing occupies 19 acres of a 33-acre site large enough to have been able to accommodate the legendary liner *Titanic* and both of its sister ships side by side. It replaced an earlier development at Normanton.

The other British locations from which Eddie Stobart operates are, from north to south: Glasgow; Carlisle's Kingstown Industrial Estate; Penrith; Leyland, Lancashire; Burton-upon-Trent; Oldbury; Wisbech, Cambridgeshire; Woolfox near Stamford, Lincolnshire; Harlow; Avonmouth (Bristol);Beckton, East London; Bridgwater; Reading (for Heathrow airport); Sittingbourne; and Poole.

8. WHY THERE'S ALSO A STOBART COACH

When a luxury coach appeared in Eddie Stobart livery — with the words 'Express Travel' displayed on the side — at the biennial Coach & Bus exhibition in Birmingham in October 1997, a ripple of excitement and apprehension broke out across the coaching world. Was Edward Stobart about to do for passenger carrying what he had achieved with road freight over the previous 27 years?

The coach — a six-wheel Volvo B12T with double-deck Van Hool Astrobel bodywork — came from two of Europe's leading suppliers and was a very special vehicle. Its normal seating capacity of 72 was reduced to just 35, as there were tables, seven television monitors and a sound system in this fully air-conditioned vehicle. It's powered by the same type of engine as the large fleet of FH12 trucks, except this is mounted at the rear. The chassis is built in Sweden, the body in Belgium.

Deborah Jane, as it's been named, isn't a threat to the scheduled coach service operators like National Express — more a reflection of the requirements of a fast-growing industrial company. It exists mainly to carry Stobart employees and customers around the country. It needs to take groups of around 20 people at a time either to visit warehouses and depots or, increasingly, to carry employees from regional depots to a central training department in Wakefield. These are journeys it's making at least every second week; previously, the company was finding difficulty always being able to hire coaches of the right standard, especially those where all the passengers could sit around tables.

Over and above the company's own requirements, Stobart's also sponsors Carlisle United football club, and the coach is available for team transport when it isn't booked by the company.

Below: Deborah Jane, the Van Hool Astrobel-bodied Volvo B12T coach numbered C000 (R12 ESL), is in a similar livery to the truck fleet, right down to the diagonal warning stripes at the front and back. It is seen here at Carlisle headquarters, between trips. *Alan Millar*